W9-CMJ-324

DISCARD

BEYOND THE ARCTIC CIRCLE

BY THE SAME AUTHOR

Air Pollution
Alaska, the Embattled Frontier
America's Endangered Wildlife
Animal Movers
Big Nick
Bird Watcher's Bible
Caves
Death Valley
Islands and Their Mysteries
King Gator
Never Pet a Porcupine
Never Trust a Cowbird
Sign of the Flying Goose
The Alien Animals
The Diligent Destroyers
The Flying Sea Otters
The Pelicans
People and Other Mammals
Squirrels
Strange Monsters and Great Searches
Water Pollution
Whitetail
Wild Animals, Safe Places
Wild Refuge
Wild Travelers
Wingspread

George Laycock

BEYOND THE ARCTIC CIRCLE

Four Winds Press   **New York**

DISCARD

J
919.8
L

38754

Library of Congress Cataloging in Publication Data

Laycock, George.
  Beyond the Arctic Circle.

  Bibliography: p.
  Includes index.
  1. Arctic regions—Juvenile literature.   I.   Title.
G614.L39   919.8   77-15844
ISBN 0-590-07481-4

Published by Four Winds Press
A Division of Scholastic Magazines, Inc., New York, N.Y.
Copyright © 1978 by George Laycock
All rights reserved
Printed in the United States of America
Library of Congress Catalog Card Number: 77-15844
    1   2   3   4   5   82   81   80   79   78

CONTENTS

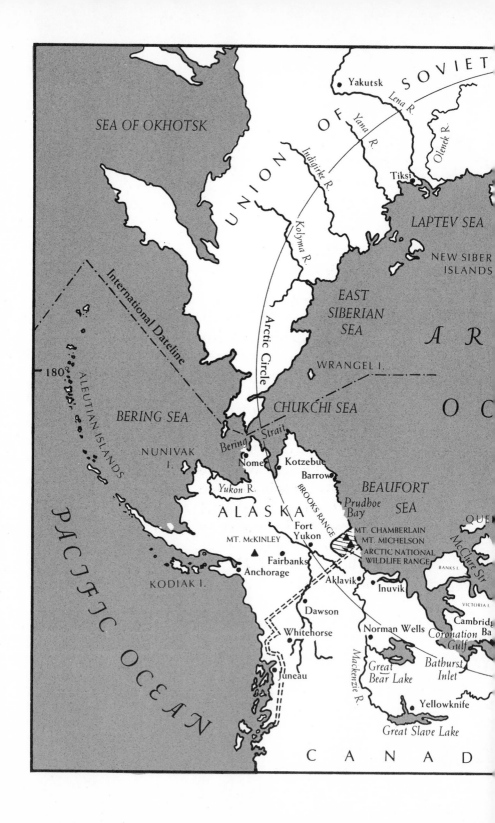

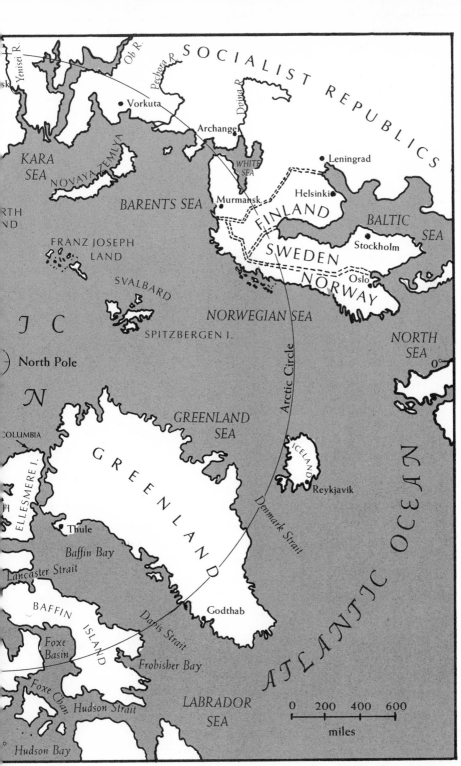

map by Gwen Hamlin

EYES ON THE ARCTIC The Arctic is the last of the North American wilderness. In winter it is a broad snowy land robed in darkness. In summer it is rolling gray-green tundra stretching out of sight. For thousands of years the moaning wind, the howl of a wolf, and the call of wild geese were the sounds of the Arctic. This wilderness was also the home of the Eskimos, a race of hunters and fishermen who called themselves Inuit, or "the People." To survive in the severe arctic climate, the Eskimos had learned to take what they needed from the land and the waters around them. The seal, walrus, caribou, and various arctic birds gave them food and materials for the clothing they needed to protect them from the bitter cold.

But the simple world of these Arctic people was certain to change. For four hundred years adventurers from the south have been drawn to see what lies beyond the Arctic Circle. White explorers arrived in great ships with tall sails. Merchants came to trade for the white fox furs and brought manufactured goods into the life of the Eskimo. Missionaries arrived with their teachings and police with their laws.

Then in the 1960s came the discovery of minerals in the Arctic, especially oil, and the changes came faster than ever. In some places the roar of aircraft filled the skies, day and night, while ships pushed north through fields of broken ice. Steel towers rose against the gray skies. For some of the Eskimos there were jobs on new machines.

As the lives of the people changed, so did their land. These changes are still underway as the North moves into a new age.

George Laycock

1

THE LAND BEYOND THE ARCTIC CIRCLE

For several minutes I lay snug in my sleeping bag, wondering what had brought me out of a sound sleep. An eerie silence was on the land. Even the arctic wind was still; not the slightest breeze moved the sides of the tent. There was no sound from the other tents nearby. But sleep did not return to me, and the events of the evening were chasing through my mind.

Five of us had arrived at the edge of the Arctic Ocean that afternoon to make pictures and search for new fishing waters for the Canadian government. Don Hamilton, our pilot, flew low across the tundra. He carefully studied the surface of the bay, noting the direction the waves were moving. This told him the wind direction, which he must know to make a safe landing. He brought the aircraft around and headed it into the wind. Then we began descending. The plane's long aluminum floats settled gently into the clear water. Don turned the plane and taxied back toward the rocky shore at the base of the sheer cliffs.

We tied the plane to boulders, unloaded our camping equipment and carried it up the slope. At this side of the bay the cliff sheltered us from the strong west wind. Also, we could look out across the water from here.

Our tents were probably the first to stand there on the Kent Peninsula for many years. There was no evidence that either Eskimos or outsiders had been here in recent times. We began to prepare the evening meal, but for this we needed fish, so I assembled my spinning rod and hiked back down the slope to the edge of the bay.

The shiny red and silver lure sailed out over the water and splashed gently as it landed. The flashing lure veered from side to side, traveling only a short time before it was struck with a savage force that bent my fishing rod into a half circle.

The fish, a beautiful silvery arctic char of about eight pounds, was all we needed. I carried it back to camp along a faint trail that had probably once been followed by Eskimo fishermen.

Thinking over these events, I was now fully awake. I looked at my watch—midnight. Quietly I slipped from my sleeping bag and dressed, buttoning my heavy wool jacket against the chill of the arctic summer night.

Outside the tent I entered a strange, ghostly world. Darkness had not come with the night. In the Far North, summer days last around the clock. But the midnight light was a dull gray light that cast no shadows. It was an hour of stillness. No loon called and the arctic ground squirrel that had scolded us earlier slept in its burrow. I had the strange feeling that I was alone in the world.

My fishing rod still leaned against the outside of the tent. I wondered if the fish were asleep and, picking up the rod, I started down to the rock from which I had caught our dinner. Once more the spinning rod sent the heavy metal lure sailing out across the bay. It made the entire trip back to me without interruption. I cast again and the immediate jolt of the striking fish jarred me back to reality. The fish was stronger than the one before, much stronger. I could feel its weight against my line as I reeled it in. Without removing the fish from the water I reached down, unhooked it, and watched it turn slowly, then rush back to deep water.

In other years Eskimo fishermen had taken thousands of these fish from this pool for themselves and their dogs.

Leaning my fishing rod against a boulder, I turned slowly and glanced at the clifftop behind me. There, silhouetted against the skyline, was a row of silent little men standing at rigid attention looking down upon the bay.

I turned to look at the cliff on the other side of the bay and there stood another row of figures against the gray sky. I had seen figures like them before elsewhere in the Arctic. They were the inukshuk, or stone men. How long had they stood guard on the cliffs? A hundred years? A thousand? Eskimos had told me that the inukshuk had a special job. Here on the edge of the Kent Peninsula, in Canada's Central Arctic, their job was easy to understand. To the Eskimo this had long been a place for killing caribou as the animals passed through in their fall migration.

The Eskimo hunters came to the Kent Peninsula in autumn to meet the wild deer of the Arctic. They brought their entire families for the important work at hand. Tuktu, the caribou, moved in broad herds inland across the tundra for winter. And in a short time the people must kill all the tuktu needed for the long dark winter.

We had seen where they once erected their caribou skin tents near our own campsite. The Eskimos had weighted down the flaps of the skin with rocks the size of a man's head, and when they left, these rings of tent stones remained behind, marking sites where Eskimo families had slept and prepared and eaten their meals during the days of the hunt.

Before white explorers introduced firearms to the Arctic, Eskimo hunters used spears and bows and arrows to kill caribou. For this they had to get close to the animals. But at this place the caribou would come between the cliffs. Perhaps the rows of inukshuk built on the clifftops looked like men and helped move the animals toward the hunters.

Hidden among the rocks, the silent Eskimo hunters waited

Stone inukshuk (which means "looks like man") built by the Eskimos are believed to have helped them drive migrating caribou past hidden hunters.

A modern fisherman on the Kent Peninsula examines the tent ring left by an ancient fisherman who used a circle of rocks to hold down his caribou skin tent.

until they were surrounded by the fast-walking tuktu, whose feet clicked and clattered all around. If the startled caribou tried to turn back as the hunters rose among them, the wives and children of the hunters came from their hiding places. They made loud noises and waved their arms while the confused caribou ran on among the hunters, who shot as fast as they could.

The dead caribou were butchered and stacked and the whole pile was soon frozen solid in the bitter cold and therefore was safe from spoiling. Such food caches were covered with heavy stones to protect them from the bear and the wolverine.

After one day we left the killing place at Kent Peninsula. Don pointed the nose of his plane toward the sky and lifted us above the wild Arctic. I gazed down upon that ancient campsite as long as it was visible. The inukshuk and the stone tent rings had brought us closer to the Eskimo people —the Inuit—of long ago. These people had learned to live in the coldest part of the world, the land beyond the Arctic Circle.

The Arctic Circle is an imaginary line around the world at 66° 30′ north latitude. On the map you can trace it across northern Alaska and Canada. Most of Greenland and also parts of Finland, Sweden, and Russia lie north of the Arctic Circle. Within this circle is the smallest of the world's oceans, the Arctic Ocean, much of it sealed in ice the year around. In the middle of this circle is the North Pole.

Two facts place the Arctic Circle where it is—the position of the earth in relation to the sun, and the tilt of the earth on its own axis. The earth moves slowly around the sun on a grand circuit that takes it a year. While it is moving along this path, the earth is also revolving on its own axis once every 24 hours. But the earth does not sit up straight while revolving and traveling around the sun. Instead, it leans to one side, tilting 23½ degrees. This means that, as the earth moves around the sun, the light of the sun falls on a slightly different part of it with each passing day. In the summer, when the top of the world is leaning toward the sun, there is light there every hour of the day and the sun does not set even at night. Then, when winter comes and the earth is on the other side of the sun, the top of the world leans away from the sun and there is only darkness upon the Arctic.

The Arctic Circle is at the farthest point south where for one 24-hour day, about June 22 every year, the sun does not fall below the horizon. On this line also there is one day in winter, about December 22, when the sun never rises.

Some might argue that there are better ways to define the Arctic than by the Arctic Circle itself. Perhaps it should be the region beyond the timberline, the northernmost limit where large trees grow. Or perhaps the average summer temperature should determine the part of the earth known as the Arctic. But instead the sun draws the Arctic Circle, and marks its line well, lighting every part of the earth north of the circle for the same number of days every year. This is the boundary of the Arctic used by geographers.

This region of the earth north of the Arctic Circle is a land of mystery and rare beauty, with bitter cold, dark winters and a rush of summer life through the long bright days. Temperatures may become surprisingly high during the Arctic summer. Temperatures above 70°F are commonly encountered by Arctic travelers. At Fort Yukon, near the Arctic Circle in Alaska, there have been official readings of 100°F in the shade. The coldest parts of the Arctic are not at the North Pole, but instead are found closer to the Arctic Circle. The coldest place of all is Yakutsk near the Arctic Circle in Russia, where temperatures have been measured at 90°F below zero.

For countless centuries the Arctic remained unchanged, and the lives of the people of the Far North were primitive and unchanging, too.

Then in the late 1960s the promise of oil and other riches began drawing thousands of outsiders north to the land of the long cold night. As people from the south invaded the land of the Eskimo, the world beyond the Arctic Circle began to change. And these changes are seen today everywhere across the North. The Arctic can never again be as the Eskimos knew it before the white explorers, the government workers, and the oil people came.

2 THE LOOK OF THE ARCTIC

In winter, when the sun stays below the horizon, the Arctic is not as dark as one might think. If the sky is clear, the moon and the glow of the stars spread a pale light over the snowy world and people can see each other clearly a hundred yards or more away. For the Eskimo this is a good season to travel and visit. The frozen snow makes it easy for dog teams and snow machines to speed over the snowy land.

But there is less snow than one might expect, because the Arctic is actually a desert. A desert is said to be any region where annual precipitation totals no more than four to eight inches. Winter brings less snow to the Arctic than to lands farther south. In this open country the frozen crystals of snow are driven before the winds, drifting and piling up against rocks and dwarf willows only to be picked up again and hurried on by the restless winds. Wherever the snow settles out of reach of the wind, it hardens into a frozen crust on the tundra. Tundra is a Lapp word for the open land above the timberline.

Then, in the warming days of spring, the snow begins to soften again in the sunlight. Ice water trickles from the thin blankets of snow and collects into rivulets, creeping over the tundra and collecting into shimmering ponds.

Water that cannot find its way into creeks to be carried

A hunter and his dog team move across the snowy landscape in late winter, when the darkness is gone and days are growing longer.

off must stand on or near the surface in boggy meadows and temporary pools. If you fly above the Arctic plains in summer, you will see thousands of these lakes, large and small. In some places they may be polygons formed into uniform patterns so that dozens of lakes with similar shapes are separated only by low dikes, looking as if they were manmade. These polygons have formed over the years as the action of freezing and thawing has moved and sorted large and small particles and rocks.

South of the Arctic much of the water coming from melting snow sinks into the earth and disappears, but in the Arctic it has no place to go. It cannot filter into the ground, for only inches below the surface, the earth is frozen the year round in what scientists call the permafrost. Permafrost may be soil and water, sand, gravel, or rock. But it is frozen solid. The thickness of this layer of the earth where the temperature is always below freezing, varies over the

These polygons near the Arctic coast of Alaska are formed by repeated freezing pushing rocks and soil outward and forming dikes.

Arctic. There are places in northern Alaska where the permafrost is 2,000 feet deep, and in Siberia it reaches even deeper into the earth.

The permafrost is easily injured. The thin layer of soil and vegetation over it insulates the permafrost from the summer warmth. When the thin soil of the tundra is damaged, the permafrost begins to melt. Instead of freezing again and healing, the injury grows larger every summer. Vehicles leaving their tracks across the tundra have started gullies in the permafrost, gullies that grow, after a quarter of a century, to 20 feet wide and 10 or 15 feet deep.

Life depends on moisture, and when there is water in the Arctic, living creatures flock to it. In spring, insects by the millions emerge on the tundra. The tundra, so barren of life in winter, suddenly awakens to the sound of bird songs and the flashing of wings. Arriving in time to harvest the insects, countless birds are back from wintering in the south. In Alaska, ornithologists counted 41 species of birds

These vehicle tracks in northern Alaska uncover the permafrost and become permanent scars on the tundra.

whose lives depend on these temporary summer ponds and the insects living in and around them.

In the boggy meadows and on the ridges piled with broken rocks, plants cover the earth. The tundra bursts into flower and brilliant color brightens the greening landscape. Fluffy white heads of Arctic cotton grass bend in the breeze, and yellow poppies, deep purple monkshood, and the tiny pink flowers of the moss campion color the slopes.

This is the tundra. The arctic plants flourish and become the source of energy for the Arctic wildlife in the same way plants do in the temperate regions of the earth and in the tropics. The cycle begins with the sun. By photosynthesis, that magic biological process within the green plants, the sun's energy is used to convert a combination of carbon dioxide from the air, and water, and minerals from the soil, forming the basic sugars and starches—which nourish the plants and which combine with nitrogen to form proteins in the food chains.

Under the harsh living conditions of the Arctic there is neither the variety of plants found farther south nor the abundant growth known in temperate and tropical regions. But still the Arctic is surprisingly rich in life that has adapted to this northern world of wind, cold, dryness, and thin soil. Botanists have found some 900 species of flowering arctic plants. For most of the flowering plants the growing season is too short for them to mature and produce seed in a single summer. Instead, they are perennials, reproducing from roots and rhizomes (rhizomes are stems or runners that form new roots when they come into contact with moist earth).

Many arctic plants have developed specialized ways to conserve moisture. They have leathery leaves, low stems growing close to the ground out of the wind, and shallow root systems that thrive in the thin soil above the permafrost. Some plants, such as the Arctic poppy, have hair on their stems that helps insulate them against the cold. The poppy, which turns its yellow bowl-shaped flowers toward the sun and gathers its warmth, is one of the rare arctic flowering plants that matures and produces seed in a single summer.

In addition, the mats of low-growing plants may actually help create in a small area their own climate, called a microclimate. The microclimate around the plants may be 40 degrees warmer than the temperature a few feet above the ground. Plants surviving today in the Arctic have changed over the centuries as the northern climate changed. Change is the key to survival of the species. As the world around an organism changes, often it too must change or perish. Many plants and animals that could not adapt have vanished forever. Those remaining are no doubt still adapting,

This flower, still surrounded by melting snow, must grow quickly because the Arctic summer is brief.

still evolving as they become more precisely fitted to their world.

This adaptation by the arctic plants has contributed to the survival of the arctic animals. But the wild creatures of the Arctic too have changed and their adaptations are even more evident than those of the plants.

The roster of arctic animals is short compared with the lists for other regions. There are two large terrestrial grazing animals, the caribou and the musk ox, and one large predator, the wolf. The barrenground grizzly bear is omnivorous (both plant- and meat-eating), but feeds largely on vegetation. Smaller plant-eaters include lemmings, which are rodents, ptarmigans (birds in the grouse family), and arctic ground squirrels. These feed their own predators, the foxes, falcons, and snowy owls.

The energy that began with the sun worked upward through the plants, was transferred to the grazers, then to the predators, and finally made its way to the bacteria that decompose dead tissue. This chain of events—the life cycle —knows no end. As surely as the sun returns in summer to shine on the tundra, the cycles of life speed up again and continue through another year. All these elements together —sunlight, water, soil, air, plants, animals, and bacteria— combine in the ecosystem of the tundra. Year after year the land of the Arctic renews itself. Unlike its parts it does not die, unless destroyed by outside forces such as fire, bulldozers, or spilled oil.

Among the Arctic's most abundant plants are the lichens. Lichens are actually combinations of two plants, algae and fungi, living together. Algae are simple plants containing chlorophyll, and fungi are plants without chlorophyll. Because both the algae and fungi benefit from this association, scientists say they form a "symbiotic relationship."

In most parts of the world lichens are overshadowed in the plant communities by grasses and trees. But in the

Arctic, where many of these plants cannot survive, lichens have space to grow and live because they are capable of surviving the cold and wind, and they do not need soil on which to grow. In fact, they actually improve soil. They produce acids that break rocks down into minerals, and these minerals mix with dead plant and animal matter to build new soil.

A lichen may live in the Arctic for hundreds of years. Or it may be eaten by a passing caribou. The lichen, also known as "caribou moss," is rich in starch, which the caribou's body can convert to energy. It is a vital food for the caribou herds, especially in winter.

The southern edge of the tundra follows an uneven line, blending gradually with thin stands of dwarf spruce. This band of half-tundra, half-forest is the "taiga," a Russian name that means "swamp forest." Within the taiga the trees are scattered. Open land between them may be bog or barren rock. This transition zone between the tundra and the true forests is more than 400 miles wide in parts of Canada and in other places less than 100 miles across. The spruce trees of the taiga may be only 10 feet high after growing for 300 years or more. They grow so slowly that the rings formed by the thin layers of new wood added each year can be counted only with a magnifying glass. Mixed with the spruce may be stands of dwarf birch, both surrounded by the gray-green patches of caribou moss and Arctic grasses.

Along most of the Arctic coast the sea freezes over during the winter, until by spring the ice may be several feet thick. But the ice does not lie quietly. Currents break it up into huge blocks and winds move it, grinding and groaning, against itself until the blocks pile up in pressure ridges with crevices, cliffs, and jagged surfaces. Even in winter the ice may break apart into leads, which are areas of open water.

Then as spring comes, the ice begins to melt and break

Ice chokes Arctic rivers, sending water into new channels and forming a braided pattern.

apart so in late summer the barges can push through, carrying supplies to villages on the coast of the Arctic mainland and communities such as Cambridge Bay on Victoria Island in northern Canada. Farther north the Arctic ice pack does not break up in summer but keeps the sea covered the year round.

In late summer, captains of ships plying Arctic waters watch for signs of danger. A cold spell may cover the water first with a thin tissue known as frazil ice. This may thicken rapidly into a sludge, which may in turn form a solid sheet of ice several inches thick. The ship still pushes through the forming ice, but every day the job is tougher, and the ship that does not steam south to warmer waters runs the risk of being locked in.

This northern ocean is incredibly rich in life. Diatoms, also called phytoplankton, are single cell plants living in water. The brilliant light of the Arctic summer starts these minute plants reproducing. Currents welling up from the bottom of the sea carry new supplies of nutrients, speeding up the phytoplankton growth until the sea is said to "bloom" and turn greenish in color. Multitudes of tiny plant-eaters, or zooplankton, begin their harvest of the phytoplankton, then in turn become food for animals large and small. Even the whales move north to these ocean pastures. The plankton-eating whales swim through the sea with their cavernous mouths open. These whales have screens of flexible hornlike material called baleen in their jaws which strain plankton out of the sea water by the hundreds of pounds. In this way the cold northern ocean nourishes the largest animals in the world.

3 THE ARCTIC IS DISCOVERED

Heavy black clouds raced across the sea toward the little ship. The surface of the dark water began to roll before the wind. The ship rose to the crests of the waves, then slid down deep into the troughs, while the ship and crew were washed in torrents of rain. For hours the storm beat upon the ship, tossing her about while the weight of the masts threatened to tip her onto her side.

The winds increased in fury, and mountainous waves towered above the ship. But Captain Martin Frobisher commanded his men to continue fighting the storm with all their skill. Then one giant wave forced the ship upon her side.

With this the crew thought the end had come. Their stricken ship would never right herself. But Captain Frobisher was not giving up. Hanging onto the ship as best they could, the crew was commanded to cut away one of the heavy masts and make the ship lighter still by throwing over cargo. Slowly she rolled back into an upright position. For the next two days the crew continued to battle the heavy seas, and at last the storm ended.

In that summer of 1576, Martin Frobisher had sailed from England on a special voyage. Men knew then that the earth was round, and they dreamed of finding a short sea route to the riches of the Orient, by sailing west. But the vast unexplored continent of North America, the New World, lay in their way. The only hope seemed to be to find a route around it. This search for a Northwest Passage sent explorers pushing deeper and deeper into the Arctic, which is why, when you study a map of the Arctic, you find that many of the place names are not Eskimo names at all. Instead, the islands, bays, and straits carry the names of early explorers, such as Davis, Hudson, Frobisher, Baffin, Foxe, Ross, and Franklin. Behind each one is a story of stark drama, bitter hardships, and usually disappointment and death.

After sailing for 22 days, Frobisher found a new land he did not know. This was Greenland, but he did not stop to explore it. Arctic winds rushed down off the icy world to the north and pushed Frobisher's ships around mercilessly in the dark seas. He came to another land which he took to be the mainland, but we know now that it was Baffin Island. Before Frobisher turned back, he discovered that people lived in this harsh and stormy land. He looked at their faces, saw that their features resembled those of Mongolian people, and believed he had sailed to a new land lying close to China. He did not know that thousands of years earlier, ancestors of these northern people had crossed the then-existing land bridge from Asia to this new continent. Frobisher took one of the Eskimos with him on his return to England.

In addition, Frobisher took some rock he had picked up in the North back to England. This rock caused more excitement than the Eskimo prisoner—a chemist who examined it thought he could detect traces of gold in it.

Frobisher was sent back to the North, but he was no longer seeking the Northwest Passage. This time he was told to bring back more rocks, as much of the precious ore as he could haul. Hopes ran high in England that Frobisher had discovered the source of boundless wealth.

On his third trip, in 1578, Frobisher led a fleet of 15 ships.

With him sailed 41 miners who were directed to establish a permanent settlement. As they sailed past Greenland, winds rose and the sea was pushed into rolling waves. Frobisher fought the storm and the bitter cold, and his ships ploughed on northward.

Then, at the entrance to the strait he had discovered earlier, he met a new enemy—giant blocks of ice were shifting about in the dark water and piling into mountainous ridges. He pushed his ships on, searching for open water, until one of them, the one carrying most of the supplies for the new colony, was caught between the fields of shifting ice. It was crushed as if it were made of paper, and sank quickly. Then another storm roared down upon the fleet and more of Frobisher's ships sank. Only the most fortunate crews brought their vessels limping back to England. The money that had gone into the expedition was lost. But Frobisher's troubles were not yet over.

Back home, he learned that the tons of rocks he had delivered on his earlier trips carried not a trace of gold! With the promise of gold gone, Frobisher could no longer interest backers in his explorations. The original purpose of his travels, the search for the Northwest Passage, was almost forgotten in the bitter disappointment over his failure to bring riches to England.

Most of the Northwest Passage still lay undiscovered, because Frobisher had not even reached the Arctic Circle. But his three pioneering trips pointed the way into the North Country.

After Frobisher the English sent explorer John Davis to seek the Northwest Passage. On three trips he probed the northern wilderness, seeking a path through the white mountains of ice towering above his ships. He listened to the crunching of the ice grinding against itself on all sides of his ship. Fog so thick his ships were hidden from each other sometimes sent him off his course. But on these trips

Davis began to study the ways of the Eskimo people and how they managed to live in this icy northern land.

What Davis learned about the North—about its weather, people, and natural history—helped later explorers continue the search for the Northwest Passage, and among the most famous was Henry Hudson.

In 1607, in a little ship known as the *Hopewell,* Hudson sailed with a crew of 12 men and a boy, his own son. He had an astounding plan in mind. Hudson knew as well as anyone about the problems met by John Davis. He knew of men and ships that had been lost in the Arctic, and the years of disappointment that had gone into the quest for the Northwest Passage. In the face of all this, he simply said he planned to sail up across the North Pole, then down into the Pacific Ocean, through regions nobody knew anything about. Henry Hudson had a brand of courage greater than most. Besides, he was a skilled and level-headed sea captain. He did not realize, however, that his plan was almost impossible. But during that summer of 1607, he did sail deeper into the Arctic than anyone had ever gone before. He reached a latitude of 80° N, a record that stood for almost two centuries. Then he was stopped by ice.

But Hudson was not beaten yet. He was back the following year, and again the ice blocked his passage.

Then on his third trip he cruised along the east coast of North America, and discovered the mouth of a mighty river. He sailed up the river for 150 miles. Today this river is named for him, and the city of New York stands at its mouth.

His fourth and final trip searching for the elusive Northwest Passage, in 1610, led Hudson back into the North Country on his ship *Discovery,* and some parts of this story are a mystery to this day. His course traced on a modern map leads through Hudson Strait between Baffin Island and Newfoundland. Hudson found the strait free of ice and sailed smoothly into an open sea, keeping the land on his left. To Hudson, sailing south with land on his left could mean only that he had finally succeeded in finding the elusive Northwest Passage for which explorers had searched for more than 100 years. But after sailing several hundred miles, he saw land appear on the right as well as the left. The *Discovery* had carried its captain and crew southward, deep into a narrowing bay. On today's map this is James Bay off the southern tip of Hudson Bay.

Hudson sailed back northward seeking open water again, but the weather brought new ice and Hudson was again unable to move. Through the days that followed, his crew realized that they had become prisoners for the winter. The food supplies dwindled until there was no more than enough for two months. There was nothing to do now but ration the food and wait out the long winter, surviving as best they could.

In June, the *Discovery* was able to break out and start the long journey home. Many sailors were ill, others ill-tempered. What happened to Hudson and others of his crew that summer will never be fully known. Hungry and desperate, those sailors still in good health must have plotted to return home without sharing the scarce food with those crewmen who lay sick in their bunks. It is believed that Hudson would not hear of their scheme, and the mutineers overpowered him and his son, who had sailed with him on all his Arctic trips, and tied them up.

The sick men were brought from their bunks and put into an open boat along with Hudson, his son, and three loyal crewmen who had tried to help them. The small boat was cast adrift.

This was the last ever seen of Henry Hudson, at least by white men. Many years later, explorers probing the Arctic heard a strange tale from the native people. Old people among them recalled stories of the first white men their people had seen. They told of a wooden boat drifting ashore. It carried two people, a man and a boy. The old man was already dead. The Eskimos looked upon these strange ones and wondered at their white skin, sharp features, and the heavy beard covering the face of the old one.

Some believed the boy might be an evil spirit. They seized him, bound him in the harness used for their dogs, and tied him outside one of the tents. There the story ended.

Gradually, interest in the Northwest Passage died down, as Europeans were busy with wars and other affairs. For 200 years little more exploring was done in northern waters. Then a new age of Arctic exploration began, adding John Franklin's name to the list of famous Arctic explorers.

4 THE TRAGEDY OF JOHN FRANKLIN

People in the Arctic still tell the story of Sir John Franklin and the mystery surrounding his last voyage to the Arctic. Dreaming of adventure, John Franklin joined the British Navy at the age of 15. When Great Britain sent out two ships bound for the Arctic in 1818, Franklin, then 32, was second in command on one of these sailing vessels.

The object of the voyage was the old goal, finding a Northwest Passage. The ships were to cross the North Pole and sail down into the Pacific Ocean. While still a long way from their goal, they were caught in the ice for 13 days. But the unpredictable ice fields opened and the battered ships worked their way out and returned to England.

The following year, Franklin went again into the Arctic. He had proved to be a good leader who earned the respect of his crew. Now the government wanted him to explore more of the coastline where earlier searches for a Northwest Passage had ended.

Franklin set out on this expedition from the settlement of York Factory on the wilderness shore of Hudson Bay. When he left York Factory, his goal was the headwaters of the Coppermine River, hundreds of miles to the west and north. By canoe and dog sled, Franklin traveled through the northern winter, crossed the Arctic Circle, and set up a base camp, where he prepared for the trip down the Coppermine. His plan was to canoe down the rapids of the Coppermine all the way to the Arctic coast, following the route pioneered half a century earlier by Samuel Hearne in his search not for a Northwest Passage, but for copper. For this, Franklin's men built two large canoes and loaded them with provisions. Franklin, meanwhile, hired an Indian to bring in a supply of food to the base camp so it would be waiting when he returned. The journey was one of the most grueling ever attempted by an Arctic explorer. For 300 miles, Franklin and his men worked their way down the Coppermine River, sometimes paddling and sometimes portaging with their canoes and supplies over the rocky terrain around the rapids.

When they finally paddled out into the ocean among the ice floes in Coronation Gulf, they turned east, and here Franklin began mapping the coastline. Day after day for the next five weeks they explored the coast until Franklin calculated that they just had time to get back to their camp ahead of winter. But turning toward the Coppermine, they encountered high winds sweeping in from the west. It was impossible for them to follow the shoreline back the way they had come. So Franklin led his men into a broad bay and up another river. This stream eventually brought them within 150 miles of the base camp at Fort Franklin, but they had to cross the rugged unmarked wilderness between the two great rivers.

They started out carrying their canoes. They expected to hunt wild animals for their food along the way, but they found no game, and each day they grew weaker as they stumbled over the rocky ground burdened by their canoes. Eventually they burned their canoes to warm themselves. During the following weeks most of the party died. Franklin, gaunt and near death from starvation, finally reached his base camp, but the food had not been delivered. A little party of Indians came to their rescue, or Franklin and his remaining men would surely have died that winter. The following summer he returned to York Factory and sailed again for Europe.

But Franklin did not consider his work completed. Again, in 1835, he turned toward the Arctic. He mapped some 2,000 miles of Arctic coast and unraveled many of the mysteries that had confronted the explorers who had searched for the Northwest Passage. Franklin was a national hero when he returned to England and was knighted for his service.

Sir John Franklin still dreamed of mapping a Northwest Passage. When he learned that another expedition was being planned by the government, he requested that he be given the assignment to lead it. Although he was then 60 years old, Franklin's request was granted.

The two ships assigned him for the voyage had already served in Antarctica. But before their northern voyage, they were returned to the shipyards to be strengthened and reinforced. They were also equipped with steam engines and supplied with coal for emergencies.

Into the officers' quarters went a library containing hundreds of books, as well as fine silver service and expensive cut glass. They were the best equipped ships, and the most comfortable, ever to be sent to the Arctic. But they did not carry special clothing or equipment for leaving the ships and traveling overland. The skilled and experienced Franklin was not expected to need emergency supplies. The one precaution taken, however, was to stock the ships with three years' provisions, most of which Franklin expected to bring back.

Confidence ran high among the crews of Franklin's ships. They were 129 of the finest experienced officers and crewmen in the British Navy. The route for the first part of the journey was already familiar to Franklin from his long years of exploration, so all he would need to do would be to find his way through the channels around the Arctic islands and sail down into the Pacific Ocean.

As the two ships sailed out of the harbor on May 19, 1845, crowds, cheering and waving, lined the shores. The radio had not yet been invented, so there was no way to hear from Sir John Franklin during the journey. His countrymen could only wait for the ships to appear again on the horizon, perhaps later the same year.

But the following winter passed, summer came and went, and the winter after that. Franklin's ships had been gone three years before the Admiralty decided to send out two rescue ships to see what had happened. Most believed that Franklin and his men were still alive and well.

After a year of searching on land and sea, the rescue party returned to England. They had not found the slightest trace of the explorer or his ships.

The following summer, ships were sent to the Arctic from both the east and west, searching for clues or traces of Franklin's ships. The Hudson Bay Company, which operated trading posts across the Canadian Arctic, sent Dr. John Rae, one of its veteran northern explorers, to probe isolated places along the Arctic shorelines.

Party after party searched for Franklin. There were 40 parties in all, six of them traveling overland. Then, in the summer of 1851 on the shore of Beechey Island in Devon Strait, an American expedition came upon an old campsite and three gravestones on which were carved the names of some of Franklin's crew.

For three more years the search went on, and not until nine years after the two ships had sailed away from England did the British Admiralty officially declare Franklin and his crew dead. A reward for information about Franklin's party, however, was still offered. Dr. Rae returned from his search six months later. He had talked with Eskimos who told of seeing, perhaps three years earlier, a group of white men moving southward across King William Island. Then Dr. Rae had found where 30 of Franklin's men had died. He was paid a reward of 10,000 pounds.

Lady Franklin, however, was still not satisfied that her husband was really dead, and she began searching for someone to lead another expedition. For this trip she selected Leopold McClintock, a young naval officer who had been part of the first rescue expedition sent out to search for Franklin. On that earlier trip McClintock had learned how to travel by dog sled, and he had continued to study this kind of overland travel and had worked out improvements in equipment, clothing, and food supplies to make sled travel faster and safer.

McClintock sailed in the summer of 1857 on a little ship called the *Fox*, with 25 volunteer crewmen. The ice, that old enemy, was the worst any northern explorer had ever seen. The *Fox* was locked into fields of floating ice for the entire winter. For seven months it drifted, moving 1,400 miles. When the ice finally broke up, the explorers expected to be crushed, but miraculously the ice released them safely, and McClintock, still determined, turned the *Fox* northward again to continue his search.

That summer the weather allowed him to explore deep into the Arctic, and McClintock left the ship and began traveling by dog sled. Three sled parties fanned out from the ship to explore the islands and the seacoasts, adding new information to what was known of these Arctic channels. McClintock's team headed across King William Island toward the scene described earlier by Dr. Rae.

Ten weeks later all three teams of searchers were back, comparing notes on where they had been and what they had discovered. McClintock had talked with an Eskimo who told him of seeing two ships off the tip of the island. The ships had been crushed by the ice and one had vanished beneath the water. The other was thrown up onto the land where she lay broken apart. White men from the wrecked ships had started walking south, dragging small boats.

So while his lieutenant had searched the area where the lost ships had been reported, McClintock turned south. He found human bones along the trail followed by the shipwrecked men. He and his men also found a pile of stones that appeared to have been purposefully stacked up, and among the stones they discovered a metal box containing a written record of what had happened to Franklin's expedition.

The arctic ice had imprisoned them. Then, as the Eskimo had reported, the ice demolished the ships. The crews of Franklin's ships began marching southward through hundreds of miles of arctic wilderness. Gradually, the three-year food supply ran out, and the starving men lacked the strength to travel. None of them made it. Sir John Franklin had died in the summer of 1847.

Although Franklin never found the Northwest Passage, those who went north looking for him added greatly to what was known of the Arctic. Little by little, the riddle of the Northwest Passage that had drawn Franklin and others to the Arctic was being solved. Today it is known that there are many channels, not just one, leading around the Arctic islands down into the Pacific. But the ice is the master of the Arctic, and ships can go only where it will allow them to pass.

Roald Amundsen was a Norwegian captain and master of a tiny ship known as the *Gjoa*. One night in 1903, 56 years after Franklin's death, the *Gjoa,* with a total crew of six men, eased out of a Norwegian harbor headed for the Arctic.

The little ship followed Franklin's route and spent the winter in a protected harbor of King William's Island. The village there today is still known as Gjoa Haven. From there Amundsen sailed beyond where all other Arctic explorers had gone. On this his first trip to the Arctic, he sailed all across the northern shore of North America from east to west. He had found a northwest passage! But Amundsen was disappointed. What he had really wanted to do was be the first person to reach the North Pole!

5 A TRIP TO THE NORTH POLE

As long as men had known of the Arctic Circle, and understood that there was a North Pole at the "top of the earth," they had dreamed of going there. But not until the spring of 1909 did anyone come close. That year an expedition was moving north led by a tall, wiry man in his fifties, Admiral Robert E. Peary. One of the people with him was Matthew Henson, a lean black man who had traveled with Peary in the Arctic before and had learned to drive dog teams, build snow houses, and survive by hunting the northern animals. For years, Peary had longed to be first to stand at the North Pole, and he and Henson had worked together so long that Peary's dream had become Matt Henson's dream, too.

Others before them had struggled to reach the North Pole, but all had failed. Among these explorers had been C. F. Hall, an American. In 1871, Hall traveled north on the *Polaris*, but his ship became locked in the arctic ice, and while the *Polaris* was held in the ice, Hall died. The following spring his ship turned homeward, but the *Polaris* became so battered by the ice that the crew began unloading her supplies onto an ice floe. Nineteen crewmen were working on the ice when the ship drifted away from it. There was no way their shipmates on the *Polaris* could reach them. The battered ship was blown ashore and the men on her later were rescued by Eskimos. The 19 men on the ice floe continued to drift for 1,300 miles, until a passing ship rescued them just before the shrinking ice was about to break up beneath them.

Peary knew the story of Hall's misfortune and of other failures in the long search for the North Pole. But he was lured by the promise of going where no one had ever gone before. For nearly a quarter of a century he had wanted to stand at the North Pole.

On three earlier trips he studied the ways of the Eskimo. They alone, of all the world's people, possessed the knowledge of how to travel and survive in the Arctic. Peary knew their tools, understood their sleds and dog teams, and had studied their clothing and their ways of finding food as they traveled. He had observed the Eskimo methods of surviving arctic storms and traveling over fields of broken ice. He began adapting these Eskimo methods to fit his own needs for a long journey across the frozen land and sea. He believed he saw a better way to plan a journey by dog sled. A small party would travel ahead of the main group. This advance party would locate the best trails and clear the path so the main group of sleds and men could travel swiftly.

On his expeditions, Peary had taken not just Eskimo men, but their families as well. While the men drove the dogs, made snow houses at the end of the day, hunted, and explored the trail, their wives repaired clothing and cooked as they had done for centuries. With each trip, Peary's moves through the Arctic became smoother. With great confidence, he made plans for his fourth trip, the one he hoped would carry him across that last white stretch of wilderness to the North Pole.

His long campaign in the Far North was costly. There were ships' crews to pay, Eskimo guides and helpers to hire, and supplies to buy. He needed a ship specially constructed for pushing through the arctic ice fields. In New York a group of Peary's admirers had followed his adventures, and now they formed the Peary Arctic Club to help him outfit his expedition. The club paid for a new ship, the *Roosevelt,* built especially for Arctic travel.

Then, on a hot July day in 1908, the *Roosevelt* left the New York harbor carrying Admiral Peary, his crew, and their supplies. In the Arctic he stopped for several months, selecting from hand-picked Eskimos as well as teams of the finest and strongest dogs in the North, and also choosing the sleds they would need to haul supplies across the ice.

Winter was the time to move in the Arctic. Peary was ready to set out from his base camp near Cape Columbia when the days began to lengthen after the long arctic night. He had chosen 17 Eskimos to accompany his own crew of seven explorers. The equipment was all loaded onto 19 sleds pulled by 133 dogs. Peary had planned his journey in every detail. As they traveled north and used their supplies, empty sleds and weary men would be sent back to the starting point. In this way the party would grow steadily smaller, and the smaller it became, the faster it could travel.

By the time he was 133 miles from the North Pole, Peary had sent every one in the group back except Matt Henson and four of the toughest Eskimos. Now the sled began to make better time. The ice seemed smoother than before. They were covering 25 miles a day and quickly closing the distance to the Pole.

On April 7, 1909, Peary stopped to determine his location from observations and he was elated—he had reached the North Pole!

For 30 hours the party stayed there making scientific measurements. When they had fixed the location of the North Pole exactly, Admiral Peary and Matt Henson placed an American flag on the site and Peary wrote in his journal, "East, west and north had disappeared for us. Only one direction remained and that was south." Looking off to the white icy horizon, they knew at last how it felt to stand on top of the world!

6
THE
ANCIENT
ESKIMOS

Ancestors of the arctic people had come from Asia thousands of years earlier when more of the world's water was locked in huge glaciers and the level of the oceans was lower. The oceans were so low in fact, that Asia and North America were connected by a bridge which stood above sea level for thousands of years. Wild animals moved across it in both directions.

People crossing to North America probably spread out in family groups, gradually occupying new hunting grounds. Over a period of thousands of years they reached North America and continued to spread southward and eastward. Eventually they occupied both North America and South America.

As the great ice sheets melted in the North, they released water that flowed into the oceans and raised their level. The Bering Sea covered the land that had once linked Asia with North America. Meanwhile, some of the animals that had lived in the North vanished, among them the woolly mammoth, the woolly rhinoceros, the mastodon, the sabertoothed tiger, and the giant elk and moose. All had adapted to the cold climates, then disappeared, perhaps because of the changing environment. Some animals, however, became the ancestors of the arctic animals we know today.

As the ice receded, the Arctic became a land where people

Older people, like this man of Spence Bay, Canada, remember living only on the fish, seals, and caribou they could kill.

could survive and, perhaps 8,000 years ago, the ancestors of today's Eskimos spread northward to live along the Arctic coast and in some places inland from it as well, though far from the North Pole. Some lived on the caribou, others on the seals and fish. Some hunted the walrus, and in coastal areas such as northwestern Alaska, they killed mighty whales.

There were three major groups of Eskimos—the people of Alaska, those of the Canadian Arctic, and those of Greenland. All spoke dialects of the same language, and all had similar physical traits. But among these groups there were also many differences in customs and ways of life. The

Eskimos of Alaska lived in the richest section of the Arctic, a region abundant in whales, walrus, seals, caribou, and birds. As a result, most of the Alaskan Eskimos, although they traveled widely, lived in permanent settlements. In Greenland also, the people occupied fairly permanent villages. But in the Central Arctic, now part of Canada, the Eskimo was a nomad, moving often in his search for food, and finding little time for anything but hunting and killing those creatures on which his life depended.

Famine sometimes destroyed Eskimo villages. The North Country is not a land teeming with wildlife except in certain times and places. The cold region of long hard winters produces limited plant life and this limits the number of grazers and predators the Arctic can sustain and therefore the people it can support.

The Eskimos were widely scattered through the Arctic in small settlements and individual families. Most lived near the sea, but some lived inland. The people whose homes were close to the ocean often lived better because the sea was a more dependable provider. In Alaska these coastal Eskimos, the Taremuit, lived in permanent villages which had chiefs who enforced the rules and led the hunts for whales and walrus.

One day in April the first whale would be seen moving through the narrow openings in the ice, and excitement would sweep through the village. For days the hunters had been repairing harpoons, checking lines and floats, and inspecting their umiaks to be certain these skin boats were ready for the hazardous work ahead.

Each crew, led by the best hunter, ran to the boats. The men gripped the sides of the umiaks and slid them down to the water. Then, singing their whaling songs, they paddled out. As his boat moved close beside a whale, the harpooner drew back the harpoon and propelled it with all his strength. He twisted it slightly as he released it so that when it struck, the head of the harpoon would turn in the body of the whale. Tied to the harpoon line were two or three floats, and when the whale surfaced again, other harpoons with more floats were plunged into its sides. This was a dangerous brand of hunting. The whalers knew that if the whale surfaced beneath their umiak and capsized it, they would probably all drown.

The whale, its escape blocked by the ice, had no place to go. When it was weak from loss of blood and the dragging of the floats, the harpooner speared it again and again with a stone-tipped harpoon, trying for the heart or kidneys. Once the whale was dead, the boats all took it in tow and pulled it slowly toward shore. There they were met by the people of the village, who congregated to help drag the huge body out of the water for butchering. Then the whole village shared the meat. Once more the ice cellars the people had dug in the permafrost with pieces of sharpened bone were filled with food. This was the high point of the year for the Taremuit.

In June and July, the walrus drifted north on the ice and Eskimos living along the shore hunted these huge beasts. Silently the umiak and its burden of hunters slid through the dark water toward the ice floe on which the walrus herd slept. Then, before the animals realized that the enemy was among them, the most skillful hunter stepped quietly onto the ice and struck as many walruses with harpoons as he could before they slid into the water.

In summer, the caribou came down onto the coastal plains. After the whale and walrus hunting was done, the Taremuit would stalk caribou. Ducks, geese, and seabirds nesting on the islands or cliffs were killed and frozen or dried for winter food. Fish were caught and dried, to feed both dogs and people. Even the little ground squirrel, the siksik, was caught and eaten and its fur made into parkas. Almost any living creature of land or sea was useful.

To many, the seal was the most important animal hunted. Little of it was wasted. The Eskimos cut up the meat for food, and used the skins for making clothing, tents, kayaks, and dog harnesses. Seal oil was used as fuel for the lamps and the cooking fires. The sinews of the seal became thread for sewing, and the intestines, cleaned and dried, could be used for covering windows, fashioning raincoats, and making the floats needed for killing more seals, whales, and walrus. Seal blood was saved to cook with meat or eat as soup. And before iron was brought to the Arctic by early explorers and traders, the people of the North used seal bones to make many of their tools.

In the early morning the hunter crawled out from beneath the warm caribou skins, where he had slept naked through the night, and dressed for the long day of seal hunting. His wife rose also and fixed him a breakfast of meat stew.

Then the hunter went on hands and knees through the tunnel at the entrance of the house and into the bitter cold to awaken his dogs. They had spent the night sleeping snug and warm beneath the drifted snow. The hunter fastened his dogs into their harness made from strips of seal skin. Then he prepared his sled, which was built of driftwood and caribou antlers. In an emergency, if no other material could be found for runners, the Eskimo knew how to wrap large fish in seal skin and freeze them to make runners. Before starting on a trip he had to coat each runner with water, which quickly froze into a layer of smooth ice to make the sled glide easily over the snow.

Once the hunter located the seal's breathing hole, he stopped far back from it and tied his dogs so they would not alarm the seal. The hunter took up his stand beside the hole where he expected the seal to come for air. There he remained for hours, silent and waiting with his spear ready if the dark wet head should appear. Sometimes he waited throughout the day without taking a seal and returned to his

Two brothers of the Central Arctic in Canada dress in their finest fur parkas and carry their family's ancient bows to show how the Eskimo once hunted.

family with an empty sled. But if he was lucky, and the seal came up, and his spear worked well, he had fresh raw seal liver for his lunch and traveled home with a seal, or maybe two or three, tied on his sled for his family.

Choice cuts of seal meat were cooked in a pot. When the meat was ready the family gathered around the pot and dipped from it, until finally the meat was gone and the pot was passed around so all could have a drink of the broth in which the meat had cooked.

The hunter's method of hunting seals changed with the seasons. In summer, he often pursued them in open water from his kayak, which was always dangerous. Swiftly and silently, he moved toward the seal, keeping the sun to his back and hiding behind the waves whenever he could. He carried a harpoon with a line attached, made of strips of seal skin. To the other end of the line he fastened a seal-skin balloon. In the instant the harpoon point pierced the skin of the seal, the hunter threw the seal-skin bladder into the water and the line uncoiled behind the diving seal. The seal soon tired and surfaced, where it could be speared again.

But much could go wrong in those few moments. In windy weather the line sometimes wound around an oar, a hand, or even a man's neck. Or the seal might turn suddenly to the other side, upsetting the kayak. Unless the hunter could quickly flip his kayak upright and untangle the line, he would drown. A dying seal might bite the hunter, or an enraged female with young would attack, ripping the kayak and sinking it.

In spring, the seals were stalked as they rested on the ice. A seal lifts its head often to study the ice fields around it where the polar bear might lurk. Then, after inspecting the area, it drops its head again and takes another short nap. A hunter could spot the dark seal easily against the ice and when he did, he would walk bent over and stand motionless whenever the seal lifted its head.

When he came within perhaps 300 yards of the seal, he had to be even more careful. The seal might become nervous and slip into the water. So the hunter lay flat upon the ice. In this position he appeared to be another seal at rest, and the success of his hunt depended on how long the seal remained convinced of this. Whenever the seal had its head down, the hunter inched forward on his belly, watching every movement of the seal. If the seal became suspicious, the hunter tried to act more like a seal. He lifted his head once in a while, looked around as the seal does, then dropped again onto the ice. Or he might, again like the seal, half turn onto his side and scratch his side with one hand. The careful stalk might continue for a couple of hours before the skilled hunter worked his way to within 30 feet of the seal and from that distance hurled his harpoon.

In the evening, the hunter's clothes had to be made ready for the next day's hunt. His wife hung his caribou-skin boots up to dry. These boots were lined with dry lichens or grass gathered during the summer. Eskimo women were excellent seamstresses, and if their husbands' clothing needed mending they sewed it, making tiny stitches to shut out the arctic wind.

For the inland Eskimos, the Nuunamuit, life was different in many ways. These were the people of tuktu, the caribou. They did not have permanent villages; they followed the caribou. Their weapons were spears tipped with bone or stone and bows made from the antler of the caribou. With these tools an Eskimo had to be close to a caribou to kill it.

The caribou were strong swimmers, but in the water they were helpless against the hunters, and the Nuunamuit drove the caribou into the lakes and rivers or caught them swimming during the migrations. Then, the hunters paddled among them in their kayaks and speared them at close range.

As the caribou migrated southward in autumn toward the edge of the timber country, they passed through canyons

Fish spears are made of caribou bone lashed to driftwood handles and equipped with curved metal teeth.

or river valleys where the hunters hid and waited for them. As long as the wind blew away from the caribou, they might not know they were walking directly toward hunters hidden among the rocks. Then the men stood among them and their arrows flew. When the hunting was good the people feasted and everyone ate all he could. Meat was saved by drying or freezing for the weeks when tuktu did not come.

When the inland Eskimo had no caribou to kill, he searched the land and water for whatever could be found, because almost any living animal, large or small, could be eaten. In summer, the families moved to their favorite fishing waters, usually a stream where char swam upstream against the current toward the spawning grounds. Then, the family set up its caribou-skin tent and staked out its dogs. Sometimes several families would fish the same stream, and the men would work together to build a stone wall across part of the stream to trap the fish. Using long-handled spears tipped with bone points, they speared the large fish and threw them onto the bank. As long as the fish continued to swim upstream, the families caught and cleaned them and hung them up to dry for winter food.

At least once a year these inland people visited the coast for a fresh supply of seal oil for their lamps. They traded with the coastal Eskimos for oil, paying with blueberries and crowberries gathered by the women and then mixed in animal fat to improve their taste. The coastal people seldom harvested berries themselves.

These northern people did most of their traveling in the winter when they could speed over the frozen snow and ice with their running dogs and sleds. They traveled often, to hunt and to visit friends in distant settlements, stopping for the night wherever darkness caught them. In an hour, two people could build a snow house, or igloo, to keep them snug and warm through the arctic night or to protect them until a storm passed.

Eskimos have always been superior hunters and fishermen. This man uses a long pole and hook to snag fish from the rapids.

Eskimo men and women spear fish moving upstream to spawn.

Building an igloo was best done by two men, one working on the inside placing the blocks, the other outside handing the blocks to him. First they searched for the right kind of snow, which they could determine by the way it creaked beneath their boots. They needed snow that had fallen in a single storm, because blocks cut from snow that had packed in layers would split apart when lifted. The snow had to be neither too soft nor too hard. Soft snow falls apart, and blocks of snow that are too hard cannot be pushed together tightly to close the cracks against the wind.

With their long bone knives the men began chopping the snow into large blocks. The first blocks were placed in a circle, and others spiraled around and around on top of these, all sloping slightly toward the center of the house to help lock the blocks in place. Gradually the blocks rose and the hole above the center of the house became smaller until a key piece was cut to fit the hole in the top of the snow house. A small hole made in the roof allowed smoke to escape.

Inside the snow house they built a snow shelf for a sleeping platform. This bed kept the sleepers off the floor and away from the coldest air, and it gave them a place to sit when not sleeping. A snow house that was to be used for some time might have a window covered with the oiled skin of a seal to let light into the home.

If the oil lamps warmed the snow house too much, the melting snow from the ceiling dripped icy water onto the family. To avoid this the Eskimos lined the snow house with caribou skins fastened together and supported by strips of hide fastened to the roof.

Not all Eskimos built their houses in the same way. Along the seacoast the homes were more permanent. Driftwood and whale ribs were used to build the frame for a house, and the walls were made of sod. Other coastal Eskimos used flat rocks to build their homes.

In the coastal villages there was a building known as the karigi, which was a clubhouse for the men of the village. In larger villages there might be several karigi, each one having regular members whose fathers had also belonged to the same karigi. In this building the old men of the group would sit around and talk, and if they had no other place to live they also slept there. Young boys belonged also, and they had their choice of staying in the karigi or at home until old enough to be married. At the karigi the boys learned the legends of their people and practiced repeating them exactly as they had heard them because this was their substitute for written history. They also learned from their fathers how to make tools and weapons needed for hunting. Even the working men of the community spent much time in the karigi, taking their nets and weapons there to work on during the day. Their wives carried food to the karigi for them during the day.

Both the Eskimo men and women wore trousers, jackets, and boots. In winter, they wore two suits made of caribou skins. The inner suit was worn with the hair against the person's skin, the outer suit with the hair on the outside. This is the best clothing known for protection against the bitter cold. Summer clothes might be made of seal skins.

The Eskimo woman used no patterns for cutting skins to the right sizes. Instead, she looked at the person to be fitted and let her eyes do the measuring. She cut the skins with a special knife, the ulu, and sewed them together with needles made of bone or ivory and thread made from the strong sinews of the caribou or seal.

She cooked over a fire made by burning whale blubber or seal oil in a shallow stone bowl that was also the lamp. Care of the fire, like sewing and cooking, was the woman's job. Staying alive in the Arctic was a job for the entire family. The woman's role was as essential as that of the man. Each new bride had a sewing kit, a stone lamp, and a cooking pot, the tools with which she would work all her life.

Using her ulu, this Eskimo woman quickly removes a seal skin.

Until recent times Eskimos disposed of their dead not by burying them but by leaving them on the open tundra.

The Eskimos had no jails and no special police, but they had rules and social customs that everyone was expected to observe. Public opinion was a powerful force, and the threat of disgrace among the people led them to obey. If one committed murder, this was usually the beginning of a blood feud, and the relatives of the person killed were expected to kill the murderer. If a man's actions became a threat to the whole community, the leaders might decide that he had to be killed.

In hard times, when there was not food enough for the family, an old person might choose to walk off into the winter to die. This would make the relatives very sad, but survival of the family was more important than the life of an individual who became a burden. For similar reasons, newborn babies were sometimes abandoned to die, and before the coming of the white man's law in this century, such a decision was left to the parents. Children were often adopted, however, if their own family could not care for them.

The Eskimos believed in magic and spirits. They believed their shamans, or priests, had special magic powers. Some shamans could speak to the god of weather or call on the spirits to bring success to the hunter. The people feared the shaman's powers, thinking the shaman could fly to the moon or change into a gull if he chose. They often hated their shamans, but they believed them and relied on them to explain events they could not understand.

Eskimos also believed that there were mysterious "little people" who came and went, but could be seen only by these gifted shamans. Many still believe this. One summer day in 1975, a group of young Eskimos went swimming in the shallow water of a bay in the Central Arctic of Canada. One of them, a bright, popular boy 18 years old, swam out where the water was over his head. He sank and drowned before anyone could help him. There was much sadness and everyone wondered why he had drowned. One elderly woman in the settlement said she knew why. She had seen what was hidden from the others. Shortly after the tragedy she had looked out across the tundra behind the camp. "I saw the little people," she told the other Eskimos. "They pulled him under the water, and there was nothing he could do about it." Her people believed her.

For the shamans and all the other Eskimos the ancient ways began to change forever with the arrival of the first strangers from outside their land. Gradually the superstitions, shamanism, little people, and even the native language are being forgotten.

THE ESKIMO TODAY

One afternoon some years ago I went to talk with Judge John H. Sissions, a large, elderly man with a kind face and snowy white hair. His office was filled with souvenirs of court cases he had heard during his years traveling around the Canadian Arctic. On one bookcase stood a collection of soapstone carvings made for the judge by Eskimo artists. Each carving told the story of one of his court cases and included among them were carvings of murder, poaching, and stealing. Looking at these carvings, Judge Sissions recalled long, cold journeys through the North to hold trials of those accused of breaking the laws.

He set up his court in Eskimo villages across the North, sometimes in schoolhouses, sometimes beside his airplane while the pilot served as his assistant. He was then the only judge in all of Canada's vast Northwest Territories, and he traveled 20,000 miles a year to hold court.

Arriving in an Eskimo village, he slipped his long black robe on over his arctic clothes. He made an imposing figure. Wherever Judge Sissions held court, he had an audience. The Eskimo people, the Inuit—men, women, and children—always came to see the show.

The judge was caught in the middle of the greatest change ever to come to the Inuit. Across the North these years following World War II were a time of transition, and the

judge stood on the threshold between the old ways of the
Eskimo and the new ways of the white people. The Inuit
were told that now, after thousands of years of following
their own customs, they must obey the white man's laws or
the white man would punish them.

But everyone learned that Judge Sissions was a friend of
the Eskimo. When he sat in judgment, he considered not
only the white man's laws but also the ancient native customs. On the floor of his office I saw the hide of a large musk
ox with long dense fur. I asked him about the animal because
I knew that everyone, white man and native alike, was for-
bidden now to kill these rare creatures.

"Jimmy Koggolak," Judge Sissions told me, "shot this
musk ox at Cape Colborne in 1959. It was against the law
and the police brought him to court. I studied the old laws
and found that a Royal Proclamation of 1763 gave the
Eskimos hunting rights." Because of this law, nearly 200
years old, Judge Sissions ruled that Jimmy Koggolak was
not guilty of breaking the modern game ordinance.

One of the judge's soapstone carvings told the story of
Jimmy Koggolak. It showed a musk ox faced by a hunter
with a raised bow. Soapstone is soft and easily carved. The
Eskimo people used it long ago for making their blubber
lamps to warm and light their tents and snow houses. Judge
Sissions pointed to one carving after the other and talked
about them.

Four little stone figures showed two Eskimo couples
carrying out an adoption. One woman was handing her baby
to the other woman. For hundreds of years before white
man's justice came into the North, the Eskimos adopted
children in this way. It was a simple plan and it worked. If
one family had too many children and another too few, a
baby was handed to new parents to raise. White man's rules,
however, insisted that this was no proper way to carry out
an adoption. First there must be investigations by trained

This soapstone carving shows the native people's old way of adopting children.

This carving tells the story of a hunter who broke the modern law by killing a musk ox.

social workers. Then there must be paperwork and legal hearings.

The police, learning of the adoption, had no choice; they arrested the Eskimo parents and told them that when Judge Sissions next arrived they must appear in his court for trial. Judge Sissions looked out over the group of Eskimos and thought about their ancient customs. He decided that the baby should stay with its new family.

Another carving showed one man strangling his father with a rope. The father had decided that his life was over, and that he was a burden to his family, so he had asked his son to assist him in suicide. The son had been raised to help his parents, to obey them and respect their wishes. He was very sad but he could not refuse to help his father when asked to do so. To Judge Sissions this was not murder.

The native people were caught up in difficult times. They were in a period of change, the ancient ways giving way to the modern. Changes would come and nothing could stop them. But the judge was doing what he could to make the transition easier.

Following World War II, the Inuit practically completed their journey from the Stone Age into the Machine Age. Traveling anywhere through the Arctic today, you find the Eskimos living much as the other people who have come north to share the Arctic with them.

Only rarely any longer do Eskimo families take their food from the land around them. They shoot seal and caribou when they can, but the young men are forgetting how to trap the white fox, hunt the seal, spear the arctic char. Dog teams are vanishing. In their places are snowmobiles, roaring and sputtering across the white hills and plains.

One afternoon at Bathurst Inlet in the Canadian Arctic I was invited to visit one of the Inuit families for tea. On the outside the little house was part canvas and part wood. It was used all year long. When winter approached, the family

Snow machines have replaced the hardworking sled dogs through much of the Arctic.

would cut blocks of snow and pile them around the house, then shovel snow on the roof for insulation. We entered by a tiny hallway that helped keep the wind and snow out when the door opened. I had to bend far over to get through the door, which was only about four and a half feet high. Inside, the parents and children stood smiling broadly, welcoming me to their home. We sat on boxes and the edge of the bed while the woman poured tea from a tea kettle into our white metal cups.

The bed, filling about half of the room, was a shelf made of wood and covered with caribou skins. The whole family slept on this bed.

One of the teen-age boys brought his guitar from beneath the bed and we listened and applauded as he played country-western favorites. After the music, the people began making shadow pictures on the wall of their home. The favorite was a running rabbit made by the same boy who played the guitar. Everyone laughed and applauded.

But that was in the summer of 1970, and since then the Canadian government has brought in new houses for these people and erected them on the shores of Bathurst Inlet and elsewhere. These neat wooden houses have modern shapes, and they are warm and roomy compared with the homes the Inuit once had. Many young people living in them are forgetting how to make snow houses.

These modern Eskimos have the same goods used by people in the south. There are radios and cable television. Homes are lighted by electricity and heated by oil, while the people sit in chairs, cook on modern stoves, and sleep in modern beds. The young people dress the same as young people in Chicago or Cincinnati, play the same records, dance to the same music, and follow the World Series. At school they study the same subjects studied anywhere in the Western world, although some students must leave their homes for the winter and go to high school in distant places.

At the Hudson Bay stores in northern Canada, or the little grocery stores in native villages across Arctic Alaska, children find the same chewing gum, candy bars, and soft drinks consumed by people everywhere. Eskimos purchase these for their children while buying meat, canned vegetables, or peanut butter, just as shoppers do in the city.

But the old ways are not quite forgotten. There is still trapping for the white fox and hunting of caribou. Some families still travel in summer to the old favorite fishing streams where their ancestors speared arctic char hundreds of years ago. One morning on the shore of a lake in Arctic Quebec, I watched an Eskimo mother cleaning fish her husband had caught in his nets. In the loose pouch in the back of her clothes her small baby slept against the warmth of its mother's body. Her other child, George, was two years old. While his mother used her ulu to clean the fish, George

Using his pocketknife, an Eskimo boy of the eastern Arctic plays at helping his mother clean fish.

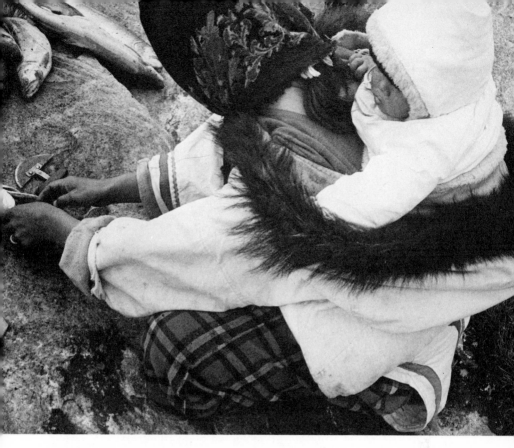

Cleaning her husband's catch is the job of the Eskimo wife. The half-moon-shaped ulu, or woman's knife, is still used across the Arctic.

When summer weather is warm and pleasant Eskimo children play on their father's sled, or komatik.

turned the head of a large char around and began prying out one of its eyes with the blade of his pocket knife. After much difficulty he pulled the slippery eye from its socket and popped it into his mouth. At that instant his mother turned to see what he was doing. She saw the eye of the fish disappear and gave George a big warm smile. She was glad he was happy and keeping himself amused. The fish eye was a delicacy for him as it has been for Eskimo people for hundreds of years.

Eskimo children have great freedom, as they always have. They are almost never punished or reprimanded by their parents, and are usually allowed to do what they want to do. I recall awakening one night in an Arctic village and looking out the window to see what was causing the noise. Three children were playing games in the half-light of the summer night. Nobody else was in sight. I looked at my watch—two-thirty in the morning. Elsewhere this would have been no time for children to play, but the Eskimo children were allowed to play when they chose to and sleep when they grew tired.

One morning in the Central Arctic the Eskimo hunters were going after belugas, the small white whales, and I was invited to go along. The belugas were abundant in the shallow cove where they had come to catch fish, and sometimes we could see several of them at one time as they surfaced and dived.

The method of hunting them was no longer what it had been long ago. Instead of a kayak these hunters used a long wooden canoe powered by a roaring outboard motor. Their modern spears had steel points, not bone, and they were attached to hemp rope, not strips of walrus hide. Instead of a float made of a dried seal skin, the ropes were attached to empty five-gallon oil cans used for floats. The hunters carried rifles to shoot the whales before rushing up to stick them with their spears. If a beluga were stuck with a spear, the floats would help keep it in sight and wear it out.

But first, the hunters had to get close to the belugas, and from the beginning, this seemed unlikely. I settled deep in the middle of the canoe, observing and taking pictures. In the stern stood my host, one hand on the throttle of the outboard, his black hair flying wildly in the wind and his face in a constant broad grin as he chased the whales, one after the other.

The whales seemed to play games with us. One beluga about 12 feet long, sleek and graceful, came to the surface to our left. Its little black eye stared straight at our canoe as if to tease us. The driver leaned the boat crazily to one side in his sudden, full-throttle turn. The canoe cut through the green water, leaving a fine white spray on both sides. But as easily as the beluga had surfaced, it now dipped back into the depths and was gone, leaving scarcely a ripple where it had been. The hunter in the bow of the canoe looked elsewhere for another whale.

This continued for several hours as the little whales surfaced and vanished, surfaced and vanished, while a dozen canoes chased wildly after them. Not a whale was touched by spear or bullet.

I wondered how the grandparents of these modern Eskimo whale chasers would have managed the hunt. For them the hunt was deadly serious. Riding low against the water, slipping silently over the ripples in their skin boats, they would have surprised the belugas and their primitive spears would perhaps have found the target. Their people would eat. If they failed there was no nearby store where they could buy meat for their families.

8

THE ARCTIC NATIONAL WILDLIFE RANGE

—Land of Wildness

Gleaming in the afternoon sun was the highest peak of the Brooks Range, Mt. Chamberlain, rising boldly against the deep blue of the cold, clear Alaskan sky. Around it were other peaks spread out into the distance as far as we could see. From our plane, we saw below us a world where men rarely walked.

In the heart of these mountains we found a narrow valley that held a pair of lakes, the largest lakes in all of northeastern Alaska. I checked the map for their names—Lake Schrader and Lake Peters. Each lake is five miles long and the two are linked together by a short, narrow stream. We glided down toward the lake with the wing tips close to the narrow canyon walls. A minute later the long aluminum pontoons sent silvery sprays of icy water up on either side of our plane.

I unrolled my sleeping bag on the grass beside the lake, with walls of rocky cliffs and mountain peaks towering above. I listened for the song of the wolf but on this night heard only the wind. There is a difference between this and other parts of the Arctic I have visited.

Elsewhere across the Arctic the oil people have sent out their surveyors and bulldozers and built their roads and pipelines. But this valley we camped in is still almost untouched wilderness. There is a reason. This northeastern

A peak of the Brooks Range is reflected in the calm waters of Shrader Lake, deep in the Arctic wilderness of northeastern Alaska.

corner of Alaska lies within the Arctic National Wildlife Range.

Early conservationists traveling into this wild land of mountains, river valleys, and coastal plains saw the beauty and majesty of the Arctic and resolved that it should be kept wild and clean. But they also understood that this is fragile country. They began talking with everyone they could corner. Far to the south in Fairbanks and Anchorage, and also in the lower forty-eight states, they showed their color slides and talked about the spectacular beauty of the Arctic. As a result the Arctic National Wildlife Range, the largest national wildlife refuge anywhere in America, was established in 1960.

This wildlife refuge reaches from the icy edge of the Arctic Ocean, southward through the rugged Brooks Range, and on to the rivers flowing southward out of the mountain snowfields. Nearly square in shape, it stretches across more than 100 miles in any direction. It is a land without roads or power lines. Nobody lives within this vast wildlife area except in the little native village of Kaktovik on the edge of the Arctic Ocean. The rest of the Arctic National Wildlife Range is left to the wild creatures. People coming here are only temporary visitors who do their exploring, canoeing, hiking, and picture-taking, then hurry south again to more comfortable climates.

As I sat one afternoon on a hill high above our camp, I could see Mt. Michelson, and I recalled a story, told me years before, of the airplane that went down on the far side of that massive, snowy mountain. The two men in the single-engine plane were U.S. Fish and Wildlife Service biologists. The pilot was a biologist who had flown for years in the Arctic. He banked the plane sharply into the mouth of a high-walled canyon and flew up along a small river. The men scanned the rocky cliffs constantly for wildlife. They saw the trails of the caribou and spotted the white Dall sheep standing on the steep slopes. Then, as they neared the head of the canyon, the pilot began making a tight turn to fly back down out of the narrow canyon. With one wing tip pointed up toward the peak, the other down toward the distant valley, the little plane whirred over the snowfields.

But suddenly the engine sputtered and the air seemed to fall from beneath the plane. Caught in a downdraft, there was scarcely time to level the plane out and try for an emergency landing on the icy mountainside. The pontoons scraped against the snow and rocks. The plane shuddered and twisted and came to rest at a crazy angle in a snowfield.

The biologists climbed from the plane to survey their situation, and what they found was not good. They knew the tragedies of other Arctic bush pilots who had died in the wilderness. But the pilot knew the country in which he had crashed. He realized that if they tried to walk out across those mountains of the Brooks Range they would never make it. There was the constant danger of snowstorms or of being caught in an avalanche. They did the only thing that promised even the slight chance of rescue—they settled down to stay with their crippled plane, hoping someone would spot them.

They carried their emergency equipment, tents, sleeping bags, and rations out of the plane and made a camp in the snow. The radio in the plane still worked, and time and again the pilot tried to make contact with other planes as the battery grew steadily weaker.

Airplanes flew back and forth across the wildlife range as pilots and friends of the biologists searched for clues of the missing men. But heavy clouds had settled around the mountain and did not lift through all that week.

The pilot noticed that every day about noon he heard a commercial airliner far overhead and realized this must be a regular daily run. The following day, as noon approached, the two men brought the battery from the plane. They warmed it beside their fire to give it added strength for one last call for help.

Then the hum of the distant plane was heard above the moaning wind. They waited until the aircraft was nearly overhead, and one last time they radioed their appeal for help. Far above them a member of the airliner crew turned up the volume on his radio. He heard the message giving the location of the lost biologists and quickly made a note of it.

On the mountain below, the two wildlife workers did not know if anyone had heard their call for help or not. Throughout that day no one appeared. But the following day the clouds began to thin for the first time in more than a week. Then, late in the morning, they heard the first faint clatter of a low-flying helicopter. The biologists looked at

The rugged mountains of the Brooks Range in northern Alaska are part of the Rocky Mountains.

This glacier in the Brooks Range of Arctic Alaska is a moving mass of ice and snow.

each other, gave a loud cheer, and began rolling up their tent and sleeping bags, ready to be lifted off. Their airplane, however, is still up on the side of Mt. Michelson.

Whenever I have been in this far corner of Alaska, beyond the Arctic Circle, I have felt the sense of humility that comes from being in a vast wilderness landscape of breathtaking beauty. I climbed one day to the top of the mountain behind our camp. It took all day for the climb and the hike back down. Gradually, as I climbed, the scene changed. When I crossed a new ridge, I could look down and see small lakes I had not seen before. There were snowfields in the little valleys, and underfoot the ground changed gradually from dry to wet as I went up the mountain. The melting snow was sending rivulets of ice water into every soggy meadow. Where the sun melted holes in the snowfield, summer flowers stood on slender stems, waving in the breeze, while bees and other insects flew among them. The purple of monkshood and arctic lupine and the yellow of arctic poppies turned the slopes into wild flower gardens.

Scientists say the climate changes as you climb a mountain and that for every 200 feet of altitude gained, you see the plants you would find 75 miles farther north. During the day I had climbed 1,300 feet, so I knew what the Arctic would be like on that day 650 miles farther north.

We flew across the remainder of the Brooks Range, headed toward the Arctic Ocean. The Brooks Range, 60 or 70 miles wide, is the northernmost part of the Rockies. These mountains reach north through Canada, then finally turn sharply westward into Alaska, where they run not north and south, but east and west. Geologists believe this range was created in past ages by giant glaciers, slowly moving sheets of ice, miles high, grinding the rocks and valleys away and shaping the earth into what it is today.

We flew down out of the mountains toward the northern

part of the Wildlife Range. Ahead of us now were the gentle slopes of the Arctic plains stretching out toward the distant ocean, with thousands of little lakes dotting the tundra.

I recalled another visit to these plains some years before. We had arrived when the plains were covered with caribou. It is here that the caribou cows come each year to have their calves. They give birth early in spring before the flies are thick, and they are out in the open where the approach of a wolf can be seen at a distance. This is one of the world's great herds of caribou, 140,000 strong. The Porcupine herd, as it is called, belongs to two countries, spending its winters across the mountains in the valleys of Canada and summers in the Arctic National Wildlife Range, which is in the United States.

The Arctic National Wildlife Range is also a refuge for snow geese. At the very end of summer the big white geese flock down from the islands where they nest in the high Arctic. They come winging in by the thousands to settle like a snowstorm over the plains. Fifty thousand snow geese spend a few brief weeks gorging themselves on ripening berries, storing energy for the long trip ahead. Then they lift from these Arctic plains and turn toward the peaks of the Brooks Range. They fly down across Alaska, then Canada, and finally reach the river valleys and lakes of the lower forty-eight states, where they spend the winter in California. Those few weeks of heavy feeding on the refuge are essential to the success of their annual journey.

If we need more arguments for saving the Arctic National Wildlife Range, consider the polar bears that come inland to have their cubs, the pale blond grizzlies that roam these tundra hills, the little bands of wolves that sing from the slopes, and the white Dall sheep that climb impossible cliffs. But most of all think of all these creatures together in an ecosystem that is pure wilderness, scarcely changed from what it was a thousand years ago.

�֎ 67

For many years conservationists have urged Canada to create a twin to the United States' Arctic National Wildlife Range. Such a refuge across the border in Canada would double the size of the protected wilderness, perhaps guaranteeing a future for the wildlife of the Arctic.

But the traffic grows thicker within the wildlife refuge. Oil people are given permits to come and search for signs of oil and gas. Mining companies send their experts to study the frozen lands for minerals.

Today the Arctic National Wildlife Range is America's last unscarred piece of Arctic wilderness. If it too is greatly changed, there will be no lands left to show us what the North was like when it was wild and clean.

ANIMALS IN THE COLD

Cold is the enemy of life. Wild animals of the Arctic are not there because they like the cold but because they are equipped to withstand it. Warm-blooded animals, with the exception of a few true hibernators, such as the ground squirrels and marmots, must keep their body temperatures constantly high throughout their lives. We know that in a cold room we quickly become uncomfortable. As the temperature falls, we go for a sweater. Medical science has found that lowering the temperature inside a person's body as little as eight degrees Fahrenheit may cause the person to lose consciousness. Once this happens, it is extremely difficult to get the body temperature back up to normal.

Some arctic animals meet the killing winter temperatures by leaving the North. Most birds migrate to warmer climates. But the mammals stay. These animals have adapted to arctic conditions in many ways. The heavy hair of the musk ox and the thick fur of the polar bear and the caribou are insulation against the world's coldest weather.

To survive, the arctic animal must be capable of two things. First, it must generate heat from the food it eats. Then, it must be well enough insulated to keep that heat from escaping. For this an animal needs many times more insulation in the Arctic than similar animals have in the tropics.

❊ 69

The snow goose, pure white with black wing tips, nests in the northern Arctic and then flies south to winter in warmer regions.

Among the most fearless of Arctic birds is the jaeger, which makes its nest on the tundra and will attack people to drive them from its nesting area.

Fur is heavy and the smaller an animal is, the less strength it has for carrying around a fur coat heavy enough to protect it through the arctic winters. The arctic hare can survive outdoors in protected places out of the wind. But arctic mammals much smaller could not live in the open during a northern winter. Shrews are snug in their tunnels beneath the snow. Ground squirrels and marmots, which are closely related to woodchucks, go underground and hibernate, thereby missing the arctic winters entirely.

Fur cannot cover every bit of the animal's body. Nose, eyes, and feet must usually be free of fur if they are to be useful. But these exposed areas must not let too much body heat escape. Scientists at the Institute of Arctic Biology at the University of Alaska learned that the feet of a duck or gull, the nose of a dog, or the legs of a caribou could all be much colder than the rest of the animal's body and still the animal would be comfortable.

These extremities are kept colder than the rest of the animal's body by a special arrangement of the blood vessels. Warm blood is carried from the heart to the feet of the gull or the flippers of the seal through arteries, while cooled blood flows back to the heart through veins. But these veins and arteries are so close together in feet and flippers that heat passes directly from the warm blood to the cold. In this way, the cold blood is warmed as it moves toward the heart. The warm blood headed for the uncovered parts of the body is also cooled in the process, and the heat it carries, instead of being lost through the cold feet or flippers of the animals, is saved and sent back toward the heart. In summer, excess heat can escape through these hairless body parts.

How an animal moves or positions its body can have much to do with keeping it comfortable. You may see a polar bear at the zoo on a summer day lying on its back with all four feet stretched out. This helps keep the bear cool, because more of its body is exposed to the air than if it curled up to sleep. Eskimo huskies, or dogs, curl up in the snow, tuck their bare noses and feet into their fur, and sleep comfortably in spite of the arctic wind.

All of the wild animals of the Arctic have adaptations that equip them for living, at least part of the year, in the coldest part of the world.

❋THE BELUGA

There is a small whale found in Arctic waters known as the "beluga," a word that, to the Russians, means white. As an adult this whale is snowy white. Flying in a plane above the shallow bays at the mouths of Arctic rivers, you may see dozens of belugas, cruising gracefully in the dark green water, where they feed on salmon and flounder. The smaller gray whales with them are their young. The calves are a dark blue-gray when born. They lose this pigment slowly, becoming pure white like their parents by the time they are four or five years old. The female matures in its third year, the male a year later. At this time the male is about 11 feet long, but it continues to grow until it is 16 feet long, three feet longer than the mature female.

These little white whales are found throughout the Arctic in North America and Europe. Belugas are at home in the shallow bays and the mouths of streams. They sometimes swim far up the stream as the tides come in, then return as the tides ebb again.

There remains much we do not yet know about the belugas. But people have known for a long time that the beluga is a noisy creature, so noisy that British sailors called the little whale "canary of the sea." Their calls can be heard even above the roar of the waves, and their vocabulary includes a variety of squeals, whistles, yelps, shrill cries, and rasping sounds which are said to help them navigate and find food. They listen to their calls bounce back as sound waves from shores, islands, and schools of fish. This process is known as echolocation.

Belugas are not preyed upon except by killer whales and man. Eskimos of the coastal villages watch for the coming of the beluga. When they can, they spear and shoot them to get food for themselves and their dogs. They once used beluga oil for their lamps. They still eat muktuk, the favorite layer of fat lying just beneath the skin.

❊THE WALRUS

The walrus is an incredible animal. The full-grown male may weigh two tons. The females weigh about half as much, or 2,000 pounds, twice the weight of a large polar bear.

An animal this size needs a lot of food, and the walrus eats mostly clams, gathered by sweeping the bottom of the shallow sea with its broad muzzle. When it finds a clam, it simply sucks it up with such force that it pulls the fleshy part of the clam from its shell.

The walrus looks a little like the seals and sea lions that are its relatives. All have hind flippers which propel them through the water. But, in addition, both male and female walruses have heavy ivory tusks hanging from their upper jaws. These tusks are special teeth used for digging food from the ocean floor.

Eskimos have hunted walrus since long before European people ever found the Arctic. To the Eskimo the walrus was many things. Its flesh was valuable food, hundreds of pounds of fresh meat. The skins were used as coverings for boats. Even the intestines of the walrus had a job—Eskimos turned them into raincoats.

Eskimo hunters long ago learned to be careful around

The walrus uses its long ivory tusks to scratch the ocean floor for food.

these enormous animals. They knew that walruses will come to the rescue of another walrus that is injured, attempting to push the injured walrus off the ice and into the safety of the water. If a young walrus is injured or caught in the ice, its mother will refuse to leave it.

Walruses are found in the arctic seas around the world. There are two kinds, the Pacific and Atlantic. The Pacific walrus is more abundant than its Atlantic cousin and has larger tusks.

Walruses migrate with the changing seasons, coming south in herds as ice locks the northern seas, then returning in spring as the seas open up again. It is in spring as the walrus moves northward past the native villages that they are met by Eskimo hunters.

During this migration the baby walruses are born after a total gestation period of 13 months. They may weigh 140 pounds at birth. For the next year and a half they must depend on their mothers to protect and feed them. The females may have only one calf every two years.

By the time the females are eight or nine years old, they have reached their full size. But the males continue to grow perhaps until the age of 15, when they are twice the size of their mates. A walrus may live to be 35 years old.

❋THE SEALS

Although seven species of seals breed on arctic ice, only two are commonly found on the Arctic coast of North America. These are the ringed seal and the bearded seal. The most common of these, and therefore the most important to the native people, is the ringed seal, which is named for the yellow ring on its coat. The ringed seal is most often found in quiet bays where it feeds on fish and invertebrates. It rests on the ice and slips into the water at the earliest sign of danger.

The young ringed seal is born in a snow cave which the mother digs with her strong front claws in a snow drift near the breathing hole in the ice. Seals keep breathing holes open in the ice because they must have oxygen when they are in the water. In her snow house the mother and her furry white pup are out of the wind and out of sight of the hungry polar bear. But the Eskimo who discovers the seal's hiding place sometimes takes both the mother and the young one.

The bearded seal is larger than the ringed seal, a giant sometimes weighing more than 600 pounds. But that is only one reason that this big reddish-brown seal has been a favorite of the Eskimo hunter. It wears a thick, heavy hide, which the Eskimos once used for making harnesses for their

A polar bear climbs from the frigid water.

dog teams, strong lines for their harpoons, coverings for their boats, and soles for their boots.

The bearded seal gathers its food, mostly mollusks and crustaceans, from the ocean floor, where it is believed to use its thick beard to help it feel for hidden food. Then it uses its square flippers to dig in the mud. The dark gray bearded seal pups are born on the ice in the spring, with a female having only one pup a year.

❋THE POLAR BEAR

Stretched on the ice the dozing seal awakens, lifts its head lazily, and searches for signs of danger. Then it lowers its head again to rest. It does not see its enemy, but the enemy is there. As the seal places its head upon the ice, a massive white bear inches forward, continuing a silent stalk that has been underway for the past hour. Again the seal lifts its head and looks, and the bear, color matched to the snow-covered ice, holds its huge body perfectly still. Then the bear measures the distance, tenses its bulging muscles and, with one flashing rush, slaps a huge paw upon the seal.

The big male polar bear weighs 1,000 pounds or so, while the female weighs 200 to 300 pounds less. For all its size and bulk the polar bear is amazingly agile and nimble. Carrying a 100-pound seal in its teeth, it can leap from the frigid water onto the edge of the ice. Or it can slip gracefully into the water and swim off with scarcely a ripple or a sound.

Polar bears live in five countries around the North Pole— the United States, Denmark, Norway, Canada, and Russia. Men have been the enemies of these arctic bears wherever they found them. Prehistoric Eskimos risked their lives

Although the polar bear has colors to match the snow, this female and her cubs cannot hide from the airplane.

hunting the polar bears. The crews of whaling ships shot them. Modern hunters have used airplanes to find them and powerful rifles to kill them for trophies and furs. But in recent times concern for the bears grew as people began to understand that they faced extinction. Scientists went deep into the Arctic to study the polar bears, to learn how many there were and where they traveled. They equipped bears with collars carrying miniature radio transmitters, then followed the signals given off by these radios so they could map the bears' travels. Gradually, they began to understand how the polar bear lives. Meanwhile, new laws were passed protecting the white bears of the Arctic.

The male polar bear wanders through the winter, sometimes riding an ice floe for hundreds of miles while he lives by stalking seals. But ahead of winter the female comes ashore and travels toward her denning area. Inland, away from the sea, she finds a hillside where she scoops out a shelter in the snowbank. New snow drifts around her den as the bear uses her broad front paws to dig out a hidden room, perhaps eight feet long and five feet high. The den may have more than one room, with a hole through the top of the snow roof for ventilation.

Here the female will spend the dark winter months as she falls into a deep sleep. During the winter she does not eat or drink, but lives on energy stored as fat. She is not truly hibernating and may awaken for short periods.

In the heart of winter she gives birth to her young. There are one or two cubs, and sometimes three. At first the cubs are blind and helpless as they snuggle deep into their mother's dense fur and feed on the rich milk she offers.

By April the family is ready to emerge into the brilliant sunny arctic spring, and the cubs get their first look at the outside world. For two years or more they stay with the female, traveling and learning how to hunt and survive in the wilderness.

❋THE BARRENGROUND GRIZZLY

Walking across the tundra, I think of the grizzly bear. I know the bear is out there somewhere. It may be 50 miles away, and the chances are we will never meet. But the grizzly could also be right around that rock pile ahead, or quietly digging for the roots of the Eskimo potato, hidden by the willows along the stream. Although these grizzly bears of the Arctic avoid people when they can, there are three situations in which the grizzly can be especially dangerous. A female with cubs may charge anything she thinks is a threat to her young. A bear that has made a kill may attack to protect its food. And a bear taken by surprise may attack. For these reasons Arctic travelers watch for bears and keep their distance. The grizzly, given plenty of warning, usually runs away.

Grizzly cubs are born while the mother is asleep in her winter den. Usually there are two of them, and they are very small for a mother so large. The newborn cubs weigh less than three pounds each, while an adult will weigh 600 pounds or more. Outside, the earth is frozen and the north wind rushes over the icy tundra, curling wisps of snow around rocks and dwarf trees, while temperatures fall to 40 or 50 degrees below zero. But inside the den, the young bears nestle into the deep fur of their giant mother, feed on her milk, and grow as winter passes and spring approaches. The mother teaches her cubs to dig for roots and ground squirrels, gather berries, and take the caribou calves. They also clean up any meat remaining where the wolves have made a kill. The cubs stay with their mother through their second winter and sometimes their third.

Biologists working in the Brooks Range learned that female grizzly bears in this section of Arctic Alaska average a new litter of cubs only once every 4.2 years and may not have their first young until they are 12 years old. Farther south, in Wyoming, the grizzly females have more young than their cousins in the Arctic. Through its lifetime of perhaps 20 years, the barrenground grizzly in the Brooks Range of Alaska may have eight cubs, while the Wyoming female may have 13 or more. The Arctic is not the best country for grizzly bears. The short growing season and limited food supplies may force northern bears to roam over 100 square miles or more in the search for food.

But who is to say that the grizzly bears farther south lead a better life? While they may occupy a land of more abundant food, have more young, grow larger, and travel less to make a living, they have met an enemy they cannot overcome—people have caused the grizzlies' extinction throughout most of their original range. And as people move into the Arctic in greater numbers, the northern grizzly too must face this human enemy.

❄THE WOLF

Once heard, the haunting song of the arctic wolf is never forgotten. It may come on the winds of evening as it did for Adolph Murie as he recalls in his book *A Naturalist in Alaska*. Murie was hiking through a long snowy day to reach his cabin ahead of night.

"Then we stopped, transfixed," he wrote, "for out of the storm came music, the long-drawn mournful call of a wolf. It started low, moved slowly up the scale with increased volume—at the high point a slight break in the voice, then a deepening of the tone as it became a little more throaty and gradually descended the scale and the soft voice trailed off to blend with the storm."

The Arctic is one of the few places in North America where the wolves still live. They once roamed practically all of the continent. Then the lands were settled and occu-

This Arctic wolf pup was photographed as it ran off to rejoin its mother.

pied by people and their livestock, and there was no longer room for wolves.

Wolves belong to the dog family. Those living in the Arctic are giants, the big males weighing 85 to 115 pounds. Usually they live together in packs. The pack may have only two wolves or there may be 15 or more. One of them is the leader. During the hunt they work together to bring down a caribou or moose on which they all feed.

Actually, the wolf may be good for the caribou—not for the individual it kills, but for the herd. In winter the caribou must survive on lichens. If there are too many caribou, there will not be enough lichens to feed them. The vegetation is destroyed and caribou starve. The wolf helps keep the size of the caribou herd fitted to the food supplies, giving the lichens time to grow.

When the female wolf is 22 months old, she will mate for the first time. At the end of her pregnancy, in 60 to 66 days, she will probably give birth to 5 pups. Or she may have as many as 12 or 13. For the remainder of her adult life she can have a new litter of pups every May, when spring is first coming to the tundra.

Pups and adults live together in a den and stay there until the middle of the summer. When the pups are strong enough, the entire pack travels over the tundra while the pups learn the ways of the hunting wolf.

❋THE ARCTIC FOX

The arctic fox turns pure white as winter comes, and wears a coat to match the new snow. Its white fur is a treasure for northern trappers, who catch it and trade the fur for the goods their families need.

But there are years when the foxes are rare and even the most skillful trappers fail. When lemmings are scarce, foxes starve. Sometimes they find other foods. Some follow the polar bears, gleaning scraps from seal carcasses. There are small birds in the tundra to take in summer. The fox may also surprise the emperor goose as it sleeps with its head tucked under one wing. But the lemmings are everyday fare and especially important in winter, when they can be dug from their tunnels under the snow.

Eskimo trappers know that foxes sometimes use the same den for 60 years or more. These old dens have many entrances, perhaps a dozen or more in use, plus others no longer used. Often the den is on a sandy knob rising above the tundra, where the foxes can command a view of the surrounding countryside. The entrances are often on the south slope where the spring sun first melts the drifted snow.

The adults mate in early spring, and the female has her young when the countryside is green with new growth, the nesting birds have returned to the North, and food is at its peak of abundance. The old foxes must hunt every day to bring food to their pups. In a normal year there are perhaps 8 young foxes to feed, and in a year of abundant lemmings there may be 12.

Both parents hunt. If the old fox finds a supply of lemmings, it may return to the den carrying several in its mouth at once. But if it has discovered the nest of a goose or duck, it brings the eggs back one at a time, carrying each so carefully that it does not break along the way.

When two weeks old, the pups begin to stick their furry little heads out of the entrance of their burrow. They are ready to begin learning the tundra life of the foxes, how to hunt and how to deal with their enemies—the wolves, bears, eagles, and man.

❋THE CARIBOU

One summer morning in Canada's Central Arctic, I glanced at the top of a nearby hill in time to see a set of giant antlers appear against the sky. A huge caribou came over the hill, followed by a second one, and both of them began trotting down the long, gentle slope directly toward us. Moviemaker Karl Maslowski was busy photographing a bed of brilliant wild flowers and I spoke quietly to him.

He turned his camera on the caribou, which came steadily closer until their image filled his view finder, and we could hear the clicking joints of their feet. Their ability to see unmoving objects is poor. When they were 20 feet away, they made a gentle turn to the side and passed as if they had never sensed our presence. During the morning this was repeated several times as other caribou came down the hill and trotted through our camp.

At times these restless wild deer of the Arctic assemble in herds several thousand strong and travel together. From a plane they look like a broad brown rug being drawn over the hills. A group of southern naturalists, spending a week at Bathurst Inlet in the Central Arctic, one day encountered a herd of 7,000 caribou passing through. This was the first time they had ever seen such a migration and they stayed through the day watching, even forgetting to eat their lunch. This is the kind of experience that can lead one to believe that wildlife is seen everywhere across the Arctic in staggering numbers. But nobody can predict what the caribou will do. One year they may pass by the thousands and the following year not come at all. Their routes change from year to year, and this is believed to give the lichens on which they feed time to recover before they are grazed again.

In spring the caribou cows move quickly toward their calving grounds. The trip may lead them hundreds of miles over mountains and through valleys. Within minutes after it is born, the caribou calf tries to stand on tottering legs. It gains strength quickly, and in a few days it is sure-footed and fast-running. By the time it is two weeks old, the calf has doubled its weight and the arctic wolf would not easily catch it. By the end of summer the calves are living on the arctic plants and no longer need their mother's milk.

After the calves are born, the male caribou, having moved north more slowly, arrive to join the cows and their new calves. For some weeks the large herds wander the tundra together. Then, as autumn arrives, they break up into smaller groups, all moving southward again, back toward their ancient wintering areas in the taiga, where the snow is not so firmly packed and they can paw through to the lichens

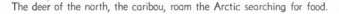

The deer of the north, the caribou, roam the Arctic searching for food.

on which they feed. Their broad hooves not only support them well on the soggy tundra and serve as paddles when they swim, but are also excellent equipment for moving snow to uncover winter food.

Caribou wear a dense fur with an outer layer of guard hairs that provides insulation, holding in the body heat. There is even hair on the caribou's muzzle. Eskimos know the insulating value of the caribou fur and for centuries have used it to make the world's warmest clothing.

The worst dangers to the caribou have been overhunting and fires that burn the plants on which they live. These arctic animals may face an uncertain future. In 1900, according to the Canadian Wildlife Service, more than two million caribou roamed the Canadian Arctic. Their numbers have since fallen to 200,000. In Alaska as well, caribou numbers have fallen. As heavy machines and thousands of oil and gas workers roam the Arctic, and snowmobiles carry hunters faster and farther, overhunting may cause caribou numbers to fall even lower than they are.

❋THE MUSK OX

The musk ox is not related to cattle, but is probably distantly related to goats. It is, however, much larger than a goat. The adult musk ox stands about five feet high. Males weigh 700 pounds, while females weigh about 450. The animal has a dark, blackish-brown fur and light brown legs. On its shoulders it has a hump and on top of its head is a set of short, curved horns with a broad base, forming a bony skullcap. The male and female look much alike.

When the earliest humans reached the Arctic, the only enemies of the musk ox were the wolf and the barrenground grizzly bear. The musk ox had its own defense against such predators. When an enemy approached the herd, the musk

The bull caribou carries perhaps the most impressive antlers of all the wild deer.

oxen formed a circle with heads and horns facing outward toward the predator, while their calves huddled in the center of the circle and crouched beneath their parents.

Eskimo hunters released their sled dogs on the musk ox trail so the dogs could overtake the beasts and make them form their circle of defense. Then, while the musk oxen were busy defending themselves from the dogs, the Eskimos attacked with spears and bows and arrows.

Then came the explorers and whalers with firearms, and the old defense of the musk oxen no longer worked. Guns could take them one by one and entire herds could be killed. Musk oxen became a source of fresh meat for the crews of the early whaling ships.

Throughout Alaska the musk oxen vanished. In Canada and Greenland, too, they became scarce, except on the lonely, barren islands of the High Arctic.

In 1935 and 1936, 31 musk oxen were taken to Nunivak

Island, a national wildlife refuge on the coast of Alaska. There they were turned free. They did well and Nunivak now has a thriving herd. Since then, other musk oxen have been released in the Arctic National Wildlife Range in the far northern corner of Alaska.

Today, where the musk ox lives wild it is protected from hunters. Small populations of musk oxen live in numerous parts of the Arctic. Perhaps the largest group of all are within the Thelon Game Sanctuary, which the Canadian government established in the Central Arctic. Within this sanctuary live about 400 musk oxen. Other thriving herds are found to the west in the Bathurst Inlet area. But never again is this remarkable arctic animal likely to thrive as it did when it had only the wolf and the grizzly and the freezing north wind as enemies.

❋THE LEMMING

In the Arctic you may catch a fleeting glimpse of a little brown mouselike rodent about six inches long and shaped somewhat like a guinea pig. It moves on short legs that keep its roly-poly body close to the ground. Little dark, beady eyes stare from its furry face. Its ears and tail are so short they are almost hidden. This is the lemming. Regardless of its small size, it is highly important in arctic food chains because it is a major food for predators, including foxes and snowy owls. One kind, the collared lemming, changes to white fur that matches the snow for winter.

Lemming populations go up and down in cycles. As long as the plants they eat are plentiful, they prosper. Each mature female gives birth to several litters during the year, adding about five new lemmings to the population with each new litter. The young are born 21 days after the mating, and in another 14 days they are weaned. The young are soon mature and the lemming population explosion continues. But as their numbers grow, their food becomes scarce and the populations begin to slide toward another low. The decrease in the plant population affects the lemmings and then spreads through the predators, too. The Eskimo trapper knows what is coming. When he sees fewer lemmings, he will soon find fewer foxes to catch.

Lemmings mostly live underground in dark, silent burrows. In winter the snow helps keep them warm. They dig tunnels that lead them to the roots and stems on which they survive. In these tunnels they have special rooms lined with grass and leaves where they sleep and have their young. They also have special rooms for "latrines." Unless the hunting fox digs them out, they remain snug throughout the long winter. Most lemmings do not migrate, but if populations explode, they may begin a mass movement, all traveling in the same direction, swarming over the tundra and swimming lakes and rivers.

❋THE WHISTLING SWAN

If you fly along the coast of the Arctic Ocean in late summer, you will see below you families of whistling swans. The adults are giant birds of pure white, larger than the biggest geese. The other swans with them, gray instead of white, are their young and they are known as cygnets. For the cygnets the world is new, and in the first blustery snows of early autumn they will lift above the Arctic marshes with their parents and fly down out of the North.

The swan family stays close together during the trip, traveling with other family groups, often in flocks of 60 or 70. Down across the tundra they move on wings spanning seven feet of sky, then over the forests, lakes, rivers, highways, and cities. Flying a mile above the earth, they travel

The chickenlike ptarmigan, unlike most Arctic birds, spends all year in the frigid North. It can walk on top of the snow and live on berries and buds.

day and night. They may fly 1,000 miles without a rest. Most swans from the Canadian Arctic spend the winter in the Chesapeake Bay country on the east coast of the United States. Another group of whistling swans that raise their young in the Arctic wilderness of Alaska fly to California for their winters.

Then in spring, the swans cross the skies again, returning to the North Country where they hatched. There, probably on the security of a small island, each pair of mated birds will start its new family. The female lays from two to eight eggs, and both parents work to rear and guard the young.

❄THE PTARMIGAN

If you were to go bird watching on a winter day in the Arctic and were fortunate, you might spot the snowy owl, the raven, and the ptarmigan. There are two species of ptarmigan, the rock ptarmigan and the willow ptarmigan, and they look much alike. Both are short-legged chickenlike birds, members of the grouse family. They are about the size of pigeons. Both are found in the Arctic around the world.

These northern grouse live on leaves, buds, and berries. They are well adapted for life in their cold, snowy land. Feathers cover their feet, toes and all. This is believed to help the ptarmigan walk on top of the snow.

In addition, they change colors with the seasons. In winter both kinds of ptarmigan are snowy white except for their beady black eyes. But in spring, as the snow melts and the tundra is a patchwork of white and brown, the ptarmigan's white feathers are gradually replaced by brown ones for the summer so the bird again matches its background. Then in fall, as the early snows begin, the ptarmigan's feathers change again and the bird is once more a mixture of brown and white. During the spring molt the hen birds may lose their white feathers faster than their mates. This helps them hide from their predators as they crouch over the nestful of eggs.

The task of incubating the eggs, perhaps a dozen or more, is carried out by the hen alone. But when the chicks have hatched, her mate comes back and stays with the family as the young birds grow. The newly hatched ptarmigan develop quickly. Within an hour or two after hatching, they can dart off through the tundra and hide from predators. Before they are two weeks old they are able to fly.

In winter the ptarmigan gather in flocks, moving into the valleys where they live on willow buds and stay out of sight in the snow.

❋THE PEREGRINE FALCON

Writers often describe the peregrine falcon as "noble," and if ever a bird deserved the honor, this is the one. It is a master of the

The peregrine falcon still nests on cliffsides deep in the Arctic.

skies. Swift of wing and beautiful in flight, it drops from the clouds with a speed no other bird can equal, sometimes reaching 200 miles an hour.

If you should see the male and female peregrines side by side, you will note that the female is larger than her mate. The male is about a foot long and his wings span 46 inches. The light-colored breast is heavily marked with dark crossbars, and the back is steel blue. On the side and top of the head are bold black markings.

Modern times have brought trouble to the peregrine. Once it lived all across North America. Then, in region after region it was gone. Scientists discovered that the peregrine's disappearance was the result of chemical poisons carried in the bodies of the birds it catches and eats, which caused its eggs to develop shells too thin to hatch. Today the only place the peregrines still nest in any numbers is deep in the Arctic. Even there the powerful birds are in serious trouble because when autumn comes, they move out of the Arctic and spend months outside the United States far to the south where the chemical poisons are still used.

In the Arctic the peregrines usually nest on cliffs. The female lays three or four eggs, and during the following four weeks both male and female take turns incubating them. After the fluffy white chicks hatch, the parents must carry a steady supply of food to them. The young peregrines grow rapidly. By autumn they must leave for their first trip south. If all goes well, they will eventually mature and return to raise young of their own on the Arctic cliffs.

❄THE SNOWY OWL

There is a ghostly white owl drifting over the tundra on broad, silent wings. Its deep yellow eyes watch for any movement in its territory. When the time comes for the snowy owl to build its nest, it chooses a place in the open tundra. There, in a shallow bowl-shaped depression on the ground, the female lays eight or nine eggs.

As the young owls hatch, the female broods them, gently protecting them from weather and predators. Meanwhile, the male spends much of his time off on the surrounding tundra, searching for food. When he is successful, he returns to the nest, carrying the body of a young Lapland longspur or a collared lemming in his bill. Or he may bring in a duck or even a fish. He leaves these beside the nest, and his mate tears the fresh meat into bite-size pieces and feeds it to the young a little at a time. Sometimes, when the male has not returned for several hours, the female calls, time after time, as if urging him to hurry back.

The snowy owl is one wild Arctic resident that you may see without traveling to the Far North. In years when lemmings are scarce, the big white owls move out of the North Country and wing down across forests and strange rivers and lakes toward the south. They fly eventually over towns, farms, and cities. If they find a place where they can catch food, they may stay for several weeks. This may be in the heart of a city, where they can live on pigeons. People gather from miles around to see the white owls at rest on a roof or television antenna. Snowy owls have been known to travel as far south as Louisiana. But well ahead of spring they are back home in the North where they will stay among the wild creatures of the tundra until the lemmings reach another low point in their population cycle.

10
OPENING
ALASKA'S
ARCTIC

As our small plane hummed over the snowy pass, we headed north toward the Arctic Ocean 70 miles away. We left the mountains of the Brooks Range behind us, flew down the long slope, across the foothills, then out over the level plains of the Arctic National Wildlife Range stretching all the way to the sea. Everywhere below us was a wilderness without signs of people or their works.

As we flew on toward the ocean I could see the white fields of broken ice, floating on the blue-green Arctic waters. The ice had been a solid sheet until summer warmth and currents broke it into drifting pieces. Behind the shoreline were shallow lagoons of quiet water separated from the ocean by a barrier strip of sand. Ducks and swans rested on the lagoons. Others flew back and forth across the tundra between the ponds.

Our pilot banked the plane toward the west and flew along the coast until we crossed the Canning River and left the Arctic Wildlife Range behind. Later, not far from the ocean's edge we came upon a strange sight, the steel tower of an oil-drilling rig. Around the tower, lengths of steel pipe were stacked. Nearby was a house trailer where the workmen lived. All around were the tools and equipment carried to the Far North aboard huge transport planes.

This drilling rig was evidence of the biggest change ever

to come to the Arctic. The year before, in 1968, a test well was drilled through tundra and permafrost at Prudhoe Bay in northern Alaska, and it struck oil nearly two miles below the surface. News of this oil discovery flashed around the world. Oilmen had gambled on the Arctic and won. On the very northern edge of North America, they had struck the biggest oil field ever found on the continent. Geologists estimated that this oil field at Prudhoe Bay might hold ten billion barrels of oil.

But the Eskimos of Alaska were not especially surprised. They already knew there was oil in the Arctic. They had seen the evidence perhaps for hundreds of years as they traveled back and forth across their snowy hunting grounds and saw where the sticky black liquid oozed from the earth. An ancient Eskimo legend told of two children who had once disobeyed their father and as punishment were cast out to wander over the land forever. They carried a seal-oil lamp to light their way through the long winter night. The oil seeps the Eskimos found in the tundra, the storytellers said, were places where the lost children had spilled oil from their lamp.

Later, Arctic explorers found these oil seeps. The U. S. Geological Survey, in Washington, D.C., knew about this oil and early in this century the U. S. government sent a crew of geologists to map these oil seeps and study the face of Alaska's Arctic for other signs of oil. As a result, in 1923 President Warren G. Harding set aside a huge block of Alaska's Arctic as a petroleum reserve for the U. S. Navy. But the oil stayed safely in the earth beneath the permafrost.

Then, during the 1960s, our need for oil grew, and the oil industry began sending geologists to search the Arctic. Most people knew nothing of this. But that changed in 1968, when people everywhere heard about Prudhoe Bay and the discovery of oil there.

Test wells such as this one revealed oil in the Alaskan Arctic, leading thousands of people north to work in the coldest climate they had ever known.

This was the beginning of a new rush to the Arctic. Many companies hurried to drill more and deeper wells on the North Slope. The following year the state of Alaska sold oil rights to a large section of the North Slope. Suddenly the oil industry had one of the biggest problems it had ever faced anywhere—how to ship this oil south to market. There were only a few practical ways to move the crude oil south —train, truck, barge, or pipeline. The oil industry settled on a pipeline, which promised to be the cheapest method. They would build a steel pipeline four feet in diameter, which would carry its load of hot oil southward out of the Arctic for hundreds of miles over mountains, across broad icy rivers, over and under tundra that had been frozen solid for centuries.

The building of the pipeline was the biggest private construction project in history. At the peak of construction, 20,000 workers lived in camps along the pipeline. For many

❄ 97

of them the Arctic climate was no problem because they worked indoors. Some did not go outside their warm construction camp buildings for days at a time. There they had recreation rooms, movies, swimming pools, college extension courses, libraries, and all the food they could eat. They also made three or four times as much money as they might have made down south, so there was always competition for the jobs in the Arctic. Some of these jobs went to native people whose ancestors had hunted caribou where the oil wells stood. Men and women working on the pipeline ran offices, kitchens, and repair shops, drove the giant trucks along the gravel highways, flew the planes bringing in supplies, and sometimes worked on top of the swaying towers in winter blizzards.

At its worst this work involved stepping out onto a derrick platform ten stories above the earth in the middle of an Arctic night when the whole world was a deep freezer. Mercury in the thermometer hung at 30 degrees *below* zero. The gale wind roaring down out of the northwest threatened to brush the worker from the tower and plunge him to the earth below. Danger lay in any of several directions. The frigid air could frost his lungs if he began breathing rapidly and deeply. The arctic temperatures and the curtains of snow could freeze his eyes shut, bringing instant blindness. Or if he were to sweat, his clothes could encase him in a shell of ice, and almost instantly the cold would chill his body so that he could no longer move.

But such jobs were vital. The machinery on the big drilling rig could not slow down. Millions of dollars were at stake. And there was always the schedule to keep. If the pipe had to be drawn from the drill hole, repaired, and replaced, bitter weather and the black arctic night were not excuses for waiting. The oil workers went out in weather that would have kept Eskimos indoors where they were safe.

The problem with the pipeline was that it could not be

built across hundreds of miles of tundra without changing the areas of the Arctic through which it passed. This land had never before been seriously disturbed by man. The wild creatures of the Arctic had wandered over it where they pleased, finding no highways, railroads, or pipelines in their paths. Theirs was a world of limited food, a wild land for wilderness animals. Conservation-minded people rushed into the discussions to do what they could to protect the wildlife and the wilderness on which it depended.

The coming pipeline brought threats of many kinds. Oil running through the pipelines would be hot enough to melt the permafrost. Methods had to be designed to put the pipeline on stilts over more than half of its length across the tundra. This meant digging 78,000 holes 18 inches in diameter and averaging 25 feet deep for the supports that would hold the pipeline off the tundra.

For this the contractors had to build special drills, just as other heavy machinery used along the oil pipeline had had to be built especially for this giant project. The pipeline had to cross 350 streams. It became the most costly private construction project ever. A truck bridge across the Yukon River alone cost $28 million. Bridges had to be constructed over other Arctic rivers, too, and a gravel road had to be built northward along the pipeline to haul materials and later to service the pipeline. All this construction required hundreds of thousands of tons of gravel. The gravel had to come from streambeds, and this would change the streams where the native fish lived.

What about the caribou, the wild deer of the Arctic? Would these unpredictable animals, which spend most of their lives traveling, refuse to cross the pipeline? In Russia the caribou, instead of crossing an oil pipeline, had once followed it right into the center of an arctic town. There they wandered around the streets, where they sometimes collided with taxicabs. Special caribou crossings were designed and built into the Alaska pipeline in hopes the animals would pass under or over the lines.

But the coming of the oil line to Arctic Alaska will, almost certainly, reduce the total number of wild animals in the years ahead, as it brings more people into the world of the polar bear, wolf, caribou, and arctic fox. People will come on the haul road created along the pipeline, for when the oil line construction is finished, the road will still be there. Crews of oil industry workers will drive it, and probably hunters, fishermen, and tourists who have never before been able to drive into the tundra of northern Alaska will follow it too, adding new pressures to the existence of the wilderness creatures.

Bringing oil from the ground and moving it to market is done at great risk to the Arctic. There is always the hazard of spilling the oil. No matter how careful the workers are and how good their equipment might be, there will surely be oil spilled on the ground and in the water. There is also the risk of oil spills—big ones—at sea, from breaking pipelines or damaged ships. Dr. Douglas H. Pimlott, a noted Canadian conservationist and an authority on the wildlife of the Arctic, has said, "It is difficult to believe that massive oil spills will not occur in Arctic waters during the next decade." Such spills can coat the surface of the ocean or tundra with dark, sticky oil spreading across hundreds of square miles. As oil spreads it coats the living creatures— the seals, polar bears, seabirds, fish, and invertebrates. Oil robs the feathers of birds and the hair of mammals of their natural qualities of insulation. The frigid water and air gets through to the skin, chills the animal, and either kills it directly or causes it to catch pneumonia. Most wild animals, once coated with oil, die.

These are some of the troubles our wildlife faces with the coming of industry to the Arctic. The American government, the State of Alaska, and the oil industry have studied ways to hold down wildlife damage from Arctic oil and gas projects. But with all these efforts the end result is expected to be lower populations of caribou, wolves, bears, and waterfowl. This has been the history of the wilderness wherever people have invaded it, and there is no reason to expect a better record in the cold fragile regions of the Far North.

But there is more to this story. Almost as soon as the oil people found oil at Prudhoe Bay, they realized that there would be another product worth millions of dollars. For every barrel of oil pumped from the earth, 850 cubic feet of natural gas, mostly methane, would be released. This fuel is in great demand in cities far to the south for heating homes and running industries. Petroleum scientists estimated that beneath Prudhoe Bay there were 26 trillion cubic feet of natural gas. There seems only one practical way to move this gas southward to the market—another pipeline.

With all this activity in the Arctic, the northern part of Alaska will never be the same again. Parts of it will be stitched together with networks of steel pipes of various sizes feeding into the big southbound pipelines. In addition, there will be highways, vehicles, people, all of them the enemies of wilderness. The natural gas pipeline is not simply buried where it is out of sight and forgotten. Instead it must have its own support system. With it must be built roads, helicopter landing pads, air strips, communication towers, and giant pumping stations that send out shrill, screaming noises across the Arctic for miles around, day and night. There must also be housing for the crews operating the pipelines. These new structures in the Arctic mean the end of the wilderness around them.

Meanwhile, the oil industry in Canada has turned its eyes northward also. Beneath the Arctic islands and the waters of the Arctic Ocean around them, there are hidden reservoirs of oil. This black wealth has lain in the earth for millions of years. But now it must come out and, because of our hunger for energy, the drilling rigs, ships, and men are moving north to bring it from beneath the earth and water. These projects are only the beginning of industry's move into the North. The future will undoubtedly bring new attacks on a wilderness that for ages has known only open space and wild arctic winds.

AFTERWORD:
Modern Arctic Traveling

More than ever before, people are going to the Arctic. Many have looked down from a distance on the tundra and the Arctic seas as they fly across the top of the world at high altitude in commercial airlines. Thousands have arrived in recent years to work in the oil fields of the Arctic.

Some have gone as tourists, but the numbers visiting the Arctic on vacation remain small. Most people choose warmer climates for their vacations. But some travelers in the Arctic want a ground-level look at the tundra and the animals living there. They are bird-watchers, wildlife photographers, and fishermen eager to see the contrasts and beauty of the Far North.

These visitors do not have many choices, because hotels and restaurants are rare in the North American Arctic. A few towns, such as Kotzebue, Barrow, and Nome on the coast of northern Alaska, have regular airline flights, and these are the busiest tourist centers in the North. People from the south arrive and the Eskimo people and other northern merchants sell them soapstone carvings, Eskimo dolls, meals, and lodging. But their visit is brief and they are soon safely back in their comfortable hotels in Anchorage.

In Canada's Arctic there are a few fishing camps for

John Nanaroak, expert fisherman, hunter, and boatman, is the leader of his Eskimo community at Bathurst Inlet in central Canada.

An Eskimo woman at Bathurst Inlet.

anglers who come to catch lake trout and arctic char. In the Central Arctic of Canada there is an unusual place waiting for the Arctic visitor—a little collection of white wooden buildings with red roofs. Flying low across the tundra you see this settlement several miles away. It sits on the edge of Bathurst Inlet, which was first visited in 1821–22 by Sir John Franklin. This was once a Hudson Bay post, selling goods to the Bathurst people and buying their fox furs in exchange. But gradually many of the Inuit moved from their homes on the tundra and settled in Cambridge Bay. Business at the Hudson Bay store fell off, and in 1964 the store was closed. Its doors remained locked for years. Glen Warner, the Royal Canadian Mounted Policeman who patrolled that lonely beautiful section of the Arctic, knew about the old store. He saw it whenever he drove his dog sled across Bathurst Inlet on his regular patrols, visiting the scattered families that still lived by hunting caribou and seals and trapping foxes for their fur.

Glen and his wife, Trish, converted the old Hudson Bay Post into an Arctic tourist lodge. Each year small groups of people from cities far to the south write the Warners at their home in Yellowknife, capital of the Northwest Territory, then join them in summer at their Bathurst Lodge. There, with the Inuit as guides, they seek out the wild animals they have never seen before and walk upon the tundra for the first time.

If you travel anywhere in the Arctic in the summertime, you need different clothes from those you wear in southern climates. When headed for the Arctic in summer, I take wool socks, long thermal underwear, and rugged trousers. I take a wool shirt to wear over a lighter-weight shirt. In addition, I have rain gear. A lightweight windbreaker or insulated jacket will turn the sharp Arctic wind. You won't find frigid weather that freezes ears and fingers, but you will wear a hat and a pair of gloves on cool, cloudy days. Good boots to keep your feet dry are especially important. My favorite boots are leather, with eight-inch tops, treated for water resistance.

If you will need a sleeping bag, a good summer choice is a lightweight down bag with two to three pounds of down insulation.

Insects can be a problem. There are days when they hatch by the millions and zero in on any warm-blooded creature. On most of these days, the modern insect repellents will keep mosquitoes at a distance, but there may be a few hours when no breeze blows and the insects give you no rest. Then a head net can help until a rising breeze puts the mosquitoes down.

Most Arctic travel is by aircraft, often small planes, because scheduled airliners reach only a few Arctic settlements. Instead of the standard suitcase carry a soft canvas bag which will fit into odd-shaped spaces.

Anyone headed for the Arctic will want to take a camera along. The secret is to cut down on weight while not leaving behind any necessary equipment. Most modern cameras carried on such trips are the small 35-millimeter models. If your camera will accept interchangeable lenses, and you have them available, I would suggest first a standard 50 or 55 mm lens. A wider angle 35 mm might serve the purpose and give more versatility. Then I would choose a medium length telephoto in the 200 mm class, and finally a longer telephoto, perhaps a 400 mm lens for wildlife. A good zoom lens can possibly do the work of two or more lenses. With this range of equipment you can take close-up pictures of flowers and medium-distance shots of people, and use the longer lenses for photographing wild animals.

If there is no exposure meter on your camera, or one you are not sure you can trust, include a dependable one in your equipment. The light will vary, and many of the days can be cloudy. The meter can save a lot of slides that you might otherwise have to throw away.

There is always the question of how much film you might

need on such a trip, and my rule is to take more than I think I can possibly shoot. You may be a long way from a photo supply shop and you may never again get back to the Arctic. Pack the whole works in a substantial camera bag that will protect it well, and take along a rubber bag or some heavy plastic bags for rainy weather protection.

Those who take a trip into the Arctic should understand that weather can often alter their schedule. There are times when threatening weather prevents small planes from flying, and travelers must accept this fact and settle down to wait. Those who have traveled in the Arctic do not urge their pilot to fly if his judgment and experience tell him to stay on the ground.

GLOSSARY

IGLOO   An Eskimo house made of snow or other materials.

INUIT   "The People," the Eskimos' name for themselves.

INUKSHUK   Stones stacked up to look like a man.

KARIGI   The Eskimo men's club house.

KAYAK   An Eskimo canoe, usually made of sealskin stretched over a frame.

MUKTUK   Whale skin, an Eskimo food.

NUUNAMUIT   Inland Eskimos.

SHAMAN   A person believed to have magic powers.

SIKSIK   The Arctic ground squirrel.

TAIGA   Region of scattered, stunted trees between the true northern forest and the treeless tundra.

TAREMUIT   Coastal Eskimos.

TUKTU   Caribou.

TUNDRA   The Arctic region north of the treeline.

ULU   Half-moon-shaped knife used by Eskimo women.

UMIAK   Large Eskimo boat made of skins and capable of carrying several people.

BIBLIOGRAPHY

Andrist, Ralph K. *Heroes of Polar Exploration*. New York: American Heritage Publishing Co., Inc., 1962.

Bird, J. Brian. *The Physiography of Arctic Canada*. Baltimore: The Johns Hopkins Press, 1967.

Boas, Franz. *The Central Eskimo*. Lincoln, Nebraska: University of Nebraska Press, 1964.

Canada Dept. of Northern Affairs and Natural Resources. *Flora, Fauna, and Geology of the Northwest Territories*. 1954.

Crowe, Keith J. *A History of the Original Peoples of Northern Canada*. Montreal: Queens University Press, 1974.

de Coccola, Raymond and King, Paul. *Ayorama*. Don Mills, Ont.: Oxford University Press, 1955.

Dunbar, M.J. *Ecological Development in Polar Regions: A Study in Evolution*. Englewood Cliffs, N.J.: Prentice-Hall, Inc., 1968.

Irving, Laurence. *Arctic Life of Birds and Animals*. New York: Springer-Verlag, 1972.

Jenness, Diamond. *The People of the Twilight*. Chicago: University of Chicago Press, 1961.

Keithahn, Edward L. *Eskimo Adventure*. New York: Bonanza Books, 1973.

Laycock, George. *Alaska, The Embattled Frontier*. Boston: Houghton Mifflin, 1971.

————. "Our Last Arctic Wilderness, A Gift Denied." *Audubon*, vol. 78, no. 4, pp. 80–102.

Marshall, Robert. *Alaska Wilderness*. Berkeley: University of California Press, 1956.

Mowat, Farley. *The Desperate People.* Toronto: McClelland and
    Stewart, 1959.
Nelson, Richard K. *Hunters of the Northern Ice.* Chicago: The
    University of Chicago Press, 1969.
Shipton, Eric. *The North Pole.* London: Frederick Muller Ltd.,
    1957.
Spencer, Robert F. *The North Alaskan Eskimo: A Study in Ecology and Society.* New York: Dover, 1959.
Stonehouse, Bernard. *Animals of the Arctic: The Ecology of the Far North.* New York: Holt, Rinehart & Winston, 1971.
Wood, Donald G., ed. *Canada North Almanac,* vol. 2. Yellowknife:
    Research Institute of Northern Canada, 1976.

INDEX

Index

Index

38754

J
919.8 L
LAYCOCK
   BEYOND THE ARCTIC CIRCLE

DISCARD